A Detective's Story

George Hatherill
of New Scotland Yard

A Detective's Story

Introduction
by Nicolas Bentley

McGraw-Hill Book Company

New York St. Louis San Francisco Düsseldorf
Mexico Panama

First edition
123456789 BPBP 79876543

Library of Congress Cataloging in
Publication Data

Hatherill, George Horace, 1898–
    A detective's story.

    1. Detectives—Gt. Brit.—Correspondence,
reminiscences, etc. I. Title.
HV7914.H29   363.2'092'4 [B]   72-930
ISBN 0-07-027025-2

Contents

Introduction by Nicolas Bentley .. vii
1) A Start in Life 1
2) Detective Training 18
3) Foreign Transactions 45
4) Three of a Kind 63
5) A Pious Fraud 78
6) Making Money 88
7) Conspiracy 98
8) The Penn Murder 110
9) In Confidence 122
10) The Alibi That Failed 133
11) Coronation Day 143
12) Operation Digit 151
13) The Great Train Robbery 165

[v]

Introduction
Nicolas Bentley

The first adult books that I remember reading were detective stories. Having once discovered their fascination (now, I'm afraid, irretrievably lost), I raced through the works of Poe, Gaboriau, Conan Doyle, Leblanc, Austin Freeman, Jacques Futrelle, and various others, not forgetting the author of *Trent's Last Case*. I read every sort of detective story I could lay hands on, but later, as I became more discriminating, I began to read fewer. My interest began to decline during the twenties, when the boom in detective fiction really began, and stories tended to become more and more fanciful and less and less concerned with reality, or even common sense. The actual processes of detection became secondary to the airing of the author's intellectual fads or esoteric knowledge. Everyone seemed to have a bash at it. Erudite men in various walks of life far removed from the paths of crime began, nevertheless, to write about it. Ladies of impeccable virtue, and consequently with about as much knowledge of crime or detection as a child has of the binomial theory, became almost overnight popular crime writers. Not one of them seemed to have the faintest idea of the grind and strain of a long investigation, or of what is actually involved in taking down and checking hundreds of statements, of the minute and methodical examination of hundreds of clues in order to eliminate all but a few, or of the close teamwork between detectives and scientific experts and others that is often the day-to-day business of solving a crime.

Undeterred by ignorance of all this, and apparently indifferent to the often brutal, rapacious, and disgusting behavior of those who commit crimes, dons, civil servants, poets, and others equally ill-qualified cashed in on the boom by adding their own ingenious fantasies to the load of rubbish that has become known as detective fiction. It still flourishes, but forensic science is becoming so complicated that no one but an expert can write about it intelligibly, and so the sillier type of detective story is giving way increasingly to the thriller, in which violence is all and intelligence is at a discount.

I have only known one detective, George Hatherill, and he is about as unlike the average fictional detective (except perhaps that he plays chess) as Holmes' enemy, Dr. Moriarty, was unlike Reg or Ronald Kray. Hatherill began life in the police force by walking a beat, and ended his career as the Commander (the present-day equivalent is Deputy Assistant Commissioner) of the Criminal Investigation Department at Scotland Yard. Under him the CID was drastically reorganized. He introduced new ideas and new techniques and doubled the staff. As a result, most Londoners still sleep soundly in their beds at night and walk the streets in daylight unafraid. It is not always so elsewhere.

Most of what a detective has to do must obviously be kept secret while an investigation is going on, and often for a long time afterwards. But without any infringement of this restriction, detectives, like other men, are prone to talk shop among their friends, especially those with the same interests. My interest in detection is not even remotely that of a professional, so I count it as a peculiar privilege that for about twenty years I have not only been able to talk to George Hatherill about many of his cases from the past, but have discussed with him at length all sorts of problems ranging from the forensic to the psychological. To the ordinary observer detection may seem to have the elements of a grim sort of game, and no one knows more about that game than Hatherill, or has played it with greater skill or a determination to win.

Detectives are not like other men. They lead in a sense double lives. Associating day by day with criminals induces an attitude towards them of fatalism and suspicion that would be disastrous if it were to intrude into a detective's private life. And not only in this dichotomy are detectives unlike other men. They often develop, as an occupational bonus, interests and enthusiasms quite out of the ordinary. Hatherill has considerable knowledge of various subjects, among them forensic science, pathology, ballistics, fingerprints, narcotics, and various processes of forgery. He also has a passion for languages—he speaks six—has traveled widely in many parts of the world, and is a student of history.

Equally important in his job has been his knowledge of human nature. To the proper study of mankind he has devoted as much thought and observation as he has given periodically to the study of tire marks, footprints, blood splashes, ink stains, cigarette ends, clothing, timetables, exchange rates, tides and currents, wind and weather—in fact, to the innumerable phenomena that from time to time he has had to take into account during his investigations. But it is chiefly in his understanding of human behavior, in his calculation of its probabilities and his knowledge of its frailties, that he has it over fictional detectives like Lord Peter Wimsey and others equally implausible. To be able to deduce that in given, though probably unusual, circumstances a person is likely to have acted in a particular way, requires first an understanding of instincts, passions, and motives before an understanding of the significance of more tangible clues. This is worth noting if only in fairness to Sherlock Holmes, who is one of the few fictional detectives with whom Hatherill has one thing in common—the faculty of logical deduction. The absurd and irrelevant uses to which Holmes sometimes put this faculty might seem to make its value suspect. But allied to an extremely practical and at the same time imaginative intelligence such as Hatherill's, it becomes a very dangerous weapon in the armory of a detective. A case that happened some years ago in East Anglia illustrates this point.

A farmer living in the Fens disappeared in circumstances that pointed to his having been murdered. Investigations by the local police led nowhere, so a report on their inquiries was sent to Scotland Yard. From his office Hatherill sent for charts of the area and for weather reports, and after carefully studying these in relation to the dossier he had from the local police, he came to the conclusion that the farmer *had* been murdered, that his body had probably been thrown into one of the dikes in the region, and that if so, it would be likely to come to the surface within a specified area and between certain dates. Holmes himself could not have done better. In every particular Hatherill was proved right, and as a result the farmer's murderer was caught and convicted.

Not every case can be solved simply by deduction. In real life, such cases, unlike those of Sherlock Holmes, are extremely unusual. Deduction is only one of various faculties that a detective needs—faculties that all of us possess, but which a detective's training and experience sharpen to a fine edge. Among these are courage, initiative, observation, and persistence. Perhaps none of these is more significant by itself than any other, but a quick eye for unobtrusive detail, combined with an occupational curiosity as instinctive as breathing, can sometimes be of very great importance. Many a crook in the confines of his cell must have regretted that his powers of observation were not as sharp as Hatherill's. A case, one of many that illustrates this, occurred during the war. Through noticing something that very few people might have spotted, or have thought significant if they had done so—which was that the pants of a dead girl lying in a mortuary were on inside out—a death that would otherwise have been recorded as due to shock during an air raid was proved to be due to an abortion.

After forty-five years in the CID, Hatherill was on the point of retiring when the most sensational crime of the century brought his career to its climax. That crime was the Great Train Robbery. Although it took place in Buckinghamshire, the Metropolitan police were very soon called in and Hatherill took charge of the case. His story of the counter-operation is one of the most fascinating of all those that he has to tell.

Anyone who has seen Hatherill on the job, who has watched his patient unpicking of the threads of what may seem to be an almost insoluable mystery, or has listened to him analyzing the possibilities in some obscure set of circumstances relating to a crime, will tell you that he is one of the great detectives of all time. This book, to my mind, leaves no doubt of it. And I should add that it is not just another selection from a detective's reminiscences. What Hatherill does is to show the extent to which modern methods of crime detection rely on an interdependence of the human senses and the resources of science. It engages the reader as deeply as he himself was once engaged in the painstaking processes of detection. It deals not only with the minute observation and comparison of data, but with the tips and hunches—and the trials and errors that are sometimes their result—and the long, hard slog involved in getting at the truth that is the real *raison d'être* of a detective's career.

A Start in Life

(1)

Fortunately for the writers of detective stories, crime has a perpetual fascination for a large section of the public. Yet in most cases there is little resemblance between the detective in fact and the detective in fiction—and for a very good reason. No one would want to read a novel that explained in detail the tedious routine that is often involved in detective work; the minute examination that has to be made at the scene of the crime; the interrogation of suspects or witnesses and the checking of their statements; the searching of records and the reading of files; the preparation of reports after an arrest has been made; and the hours spent at police and trial courts. Yet it is in carrying out tasks such as these that a detective spends much of his time. For every hour that is spent in examining clues and assessing their significance, a day may be spent on the laborious job of interviewing. From everyone who knows or may have seen something relevant to a crime, a written

[1]

record must be taken of exactly what that person has to say. Sometimes there may eventually be as many as a hundred statements or even more, some of them running to as many as thirty or forty pages. All these have to be checked one against the other. But you don't read of anything like this happening in a detective story, which usually ends with the exposure of the criminal; in real life there begins at this point a second phase of the investigating officer's job, which is the monotony of court work. There are, of course, periods of absorbing interest and occasionally of some excitement, but to concentrate on these would falsify the picture that I aim to give of what is really involved in being a detective.

A detective's career is possibly one of the most fascinating that a man can follow. Basically it is concerned with human behavior and the aberrations of individuals to whom the habits and moral conventions of civilized society mean nothing. It is far from being an easy life and I should say that most cases depend for their solution on a mixture of 98 percent of hard work and 2 percent of luck. Like most highly specialized occupations, detection requires intensive training of certain faculties which all of us possess but which few have to put to such exact use as they are put in detecting crime. Of these faculties I would say the most important are observation, deduction, and memory. It is the interaction of these three that enables the detective in charge of a case to observe the significance of factors that to a layman might seem of no importance. There is nothing miraculous about this. Given that these faculties have been sharpened by training, experience will sharpen them still further, and this will be backed by specialized knowledge, in particular, of the resources—and limitations—of the law, and by some understanding of the processes of forensic science. The growing complexity of this vital adjunct means that the hard-working detective must place increasing faith in its findings. Nevertheless, forensic science must always remain the detective's servant; it must never become his master. The infrared camera, the electron microscope, and the computer may point the way to a possible solution, but they cannot relate their own findings or results to information available from other sources, and it is upon the picture as a whole that the officer in charge of a case must base his assumptions and decide on his course of action.

In acquiring a knowledge of the subjects essential to his training, a detective is bound to learn a good deal about other things which not infrequently are rather beyond the range of most people's day-to-day activities. Among those subjects of which necessity forced me to acquire some knowledge—knowing literally nothing of them to begin with—were pathology, physiology, fingerprints, ballistics, printing, meteorology, accountancy, photography, and microscopy. I also found it necessary to acquire some understanding of various manufacturing and industrial processes. Inevitably, one learns too about the practices and traditions in a variety of trades and professions, as well as about the habits and customs of particular groups within society, such as nonwhite, racially mixed communities, religious sects, and others, not to mention criminals. The life of a detective, in fact, is in itself a specialized education. It teaches more perhaps than most professions about the general run of human nature, and so cultivates the perception essential to understanding criminal behavior.

This book is not so much an autobiography as an attempt to show what the working life of a detective is like, involving as it does the sacrifices and frustrations, as well as the satisfactions and rewards, of a dedicated existence. Few people seem to have more than a very hazy idea of how a detective is trained, how his mind operates, or how he approaches the problems involved in getting at hidden truth, which is the essence of his job. But before dealing with these matters, it may be as well for me to explain briefly how I came to choose that career, or to be more accurate, how I found my way into it almost, as you might say, unintentionally.

I was fortunate in being born in London at the end of the last century. My home was in Dulwich in southeast London and public transport in those days was cheap—a halfpenny a mile—and a penny ticket on a horse bus or a tram took you a long way. I used to profit by this to travel about all over the place, to museums, art galleries, and historic buildings, being, as most young boys are, of an inquisitive turn of mind. Many years later, in 1949, I was deputed to look into security arrangements in those same museums and galleries, as well as at Buckingham Palace and the Tower of London, where later on I was concerned in the replanning of the Jewel House.

As a boy I spent a good deal of time exploring London on foot as well as by bus, and the close acquaintance that I made with the city in those days was to be invaluable to me thirty years later when I came to take charge of the CID, first in the East End and then in the West End of London.

In Peckham Road we had an excellent local library and I made good use of it to read books about other countries and their history. Occasionally I met a boy there with whom I exchanged opinions. Forty years later I became a devoted reader of his books. His name was C. S. Forester. One thing on which I was keen at school was languages and I was lucky in having a very good French teacher, so that by the time I was twelve I could read French books with as much enjoyment as English. This encouraged me to start learning German, and by degrees I found that I had a natural aptitude for languages, which I took to learning not with any particular purpose in mind, but simply because I enjoyed doing so.

As it happened, I could hardly have chosen anything calculated to become more useful to me. Not only has it increased the pleasure of traveling abroad and being able to read books in their original language; it has also given me a very great advantage in being able to speak to and interrogate foreigners in their own languages instead of through an interpreter, who, however good, can never convey precisely the tone, the emphasis, or the inflection that often indicates so much in direct conversation. What is even more important is that I was able to develop my own train of thought in the language of the person I was talking to, which it is quite impossible to do through an interpreter.

In 1911, at the age of thirteen, I was given a bicycle and as a result was able not only to explore London more extensively, but also to start going farther afield. Pretty soon I was making trips to places well beyond London. I often rode to Brighton and in those days it was a pleasure to do so. From Streatham onwards there was open country or small towns. In 1959, I found myself in Brighton once again, this time on a very different mission: to investigate charges of corruption in the Brighton police force. It was an invidious assignment. The possibility that through my findings the careers and reputations of men of my own profession might be utterly destroyed was not a pleasant thought. I remember, after interviewing the Chief Constable, leaving police headquarters and walking down to the promenade. There I stopped, quite without thinking, exactly at the spot by the Palace Pier where I remembered having stood forty-eight years earlier, with my bicycle propped against the railings, looking out to sea and feeling very pleased with life. In the recollection of that moment it occurred to me how much of my early life seemed to have been an unconscious preparation for the career I was to adopt later on.

My first trip abroad was in 1913, when I went to Brussels, another youthful event that foreshadowed later activities, for from 1925 to 1931, I was liaison officer between the British and Belgian police, spending my time chiefly in Brussels and Antwerp, where among other matters I was helping to suppress traffic in drugs and arms. On this first visit in 1913, no passport was necessary, and I paid 10s 6d for a round-trip ticket from St. Katherine's Wharf near Tower Bridge to Ostend.

The following year I went to Paris, though after seeing all I had gone to see, I came to the conclusion that I preferred Brussels. During this visit I wanted particularly to see the Conciergerie, for its association with the events of the French Revolution, so I joined a queue outside and waited for the doors to open; I was a bit puzzled to find myself the only male in the queue. My French was not then equal to the *argot* of the women who were waiting with me and I was slightly embarrassed to notice that my presence seemed to cause them so much amusement that I eventually went away without waiting for the queue to be admitted. The next day I decided to make another visit and went in by a different entrance. I happened to mention this incident when I was in Paris again some twenty years later as I crossed the courtyard of the Conciergerie with a Commissaire of Police. Only then did I learn why my presence had caused so much merriment in 1914. The queue that I had joined was not that of visitors to the prison, but of *filles de joie* registered with the police, who were there for their biweekly VD checkup.

In 1916, after several futile attempts to join the army, my youthful appearance suggesting that I was a good deal younger than I was (not quite eighteen), I enlisted in a Territorial regiment. Again, it was as much my curiosity as anything else that resulted in my doing so. I was walking along Whitehall and happened to notice a soldier wearing a uniform with a black cap badge and black buttons. This absence of spit and polish attracted me and I stopped him to ask the name of his regiment. It was Queen Victoria's Rifles. I went along at once to regimental headquarters at Davies Street in the heart of Mayfair and, much to my surprise, was enlisted immeidately with no formalities and only for the duration of the war.

Descriptions of the mud and blood of France and Flanders are too well known for another account of them to be necessary, nor were my experiences different from those of any other infantryman. Although I was wounded, I was fortunate in not being maimed or mutilated.

When the Armistice came I was in no particular hurry to leave the army, although I had never thought of it as a career. In February 1919, my battalion moved forward as part of the army of occupation in Germany. This provided me with an opportunity during my leave to travel in Belgium, France, and Germany, and I was engaged from time to time as battalion interpreter. The Territorial battalions of the army of occupation were demobilized towards the end of 1919. My discharge came in October and I was put in charge of a group of 140 men with orders to take them back from where we were stationed in Cologne to the demobilization center in England, which was at the Crystal Palace.

We traveled by train in cars bearing the mystic inscription known to every soldier who served in France, 8 *chevaux—40 hommes.* I think we must have been shunted into every siding between Cologne and Calais. The journey took eighteen days, some of which we spent without moving. During these stationary periods various members of the party, bored with their enforced inactivity, got out of the train and disappeared. On arriving at Calais I called the roll and found that I was short of more than thirty men. That night we spent in a camp and when I called the roll again next morning before embarking in the ship that was to take us to Dover, we were down to ninety-one men. My anxiety at this state of affairs was needless. No one at the Crystal Palace showed any concern at the discrepancy between the official tally and the number of those who had turned up. The chief concern seemed to be to get rid of us as quickly as possible. Demobilization papers, a ration book, a railway voucher, and a modest sum in cash—each of us got the same, and except for our uniforms (we had nothing else to wear) we were now in the same situation as other civilians, except that very few of us had any idea of what our immediate job prospects were. I certainly had not. All I knew was that I would have to find employment pretty quickly.

It was Saturday, October 10, when I arrived home. On the following Monday I went to see a friend of mine who worked in a city office. By what I thought at the time to be great good luck, he arranged for me to go into the accounts department and on Wednesday, still wearing my uniform (I had outgrown all my civilian clothes) I started work.

I suppose I should have felt grateful, but after my first day I was dispirited by the thought of the monotonous journey that I should have to make every day by bus from Camberwell, where I was living, to the Monument (commemorating the Great Fire of 1666) and back, and I was frankly appalled at the prospect of having to spend the rest of my life poring over pages of figures. I knew it wouldn't work, but had no idea what to do instead.

Two days after I had started the job, while I was waiting for a bus, I began talking to a policeman. I told him how fed up I was after having had such a happy time in the army following the Armistice and in the course of conversation I said that I could speak French and German fairly well. He then told me about the Special Branch of the police force in which linguists were employed and suggested that I should apply to join it. So the next day I went to New Scotland Yard and made inquiries. I was told among other things that before I could be considered for any sort of departmental work I would have to serve two years as a constable on the beat. With only the haziest idea of what else was involved in being a policeman, I applied there and then to join the force, and without waiting to know whether my application would be accepted, I went back to the office and gave in my notice.

On February 2, 1920, after two months' training, I was sworn in as a police constable and posted to St. John's Wood police station.

Before joining the army I had taken a year's course in shorthand and typing with a vague idea that sooner or later they might be useful. Now, hearing that shorthand was also one of the qualifications required in the Special Branch, which is concerned largely with security matters and the protection of VIPs, I started going regularly to church in order to improve my speed by taking down the sermons. This burst of religious fervor was duly rewarded. Ten weeks after I had joined the force, applications were invited for vacancies in the Special Branch. Although I had hardly begun walking the beat, I decided to apply, to the astonishment of my superiors, who said to me openly that to make an application with so short a record of service was impudent. However, my application went in, and in due course I was told to report for an examination. This turned out to be a stiff competitive affair, but to everyone's surprise at St. John's Wood, I was eventually informed that I had passed and was transferred to the Special Branch.

For five years thereafter I was engaged in the general duties of the Branch. Then I was given the choice of being posted either to Paris or Brussels. In both of these cities a senior Special Branch officer from the Yard was stationed and was assisted by a junior. Their duties could be described broadly as cooperating with the two countries' criminal police and security forces. I had no hesitation in choosing Brussels, having been there so many times, and although I was told my posting would be for only two years, I remained there in fact for seven.

On my leave periods, as I had no particular desire to return to England, I spent my time traveling about various European countries, including those of Scandinavia.

When I returned to England in 1931, I was beginning to feel that I would like a change from the work of the Special Branch. By those who belong to it, the Special Branch is considered, as is any regiment of the Guards by its officers, to be something of an élite force, and I was strongly advised, not only by my colleagues but by the senior officer in charge, that to leave the Branch in favor of the Criminal Investigation Department, where I thought the work might be more interesting, would be a grave mistake which might affect my chances of promotion. I am glad to say these fears were unfounded. I did leave and achieved within the next seven years rapid promotion through the ranks.

Knowing almost nothing of CID work, before applying to join that department, I spent some four months in studying criminal law, criminal court procedure, and methods of criminal investigation, all of which were for the most part very different from the sort of work I had become accustomed to abroad.

I was appointed to the CID in 1932 and from then on I was frequently sent abroad in connection with cases requiring the help of foreign police forces. One such, in 1933, was probably the first case of a crime committed in the air. A Frenchwoman called Madame Schmeder had shot and killed her lover from the rear seat of a small plane. She knew how to fly the plane and had brought it down near Versailles where she dumped the body and then took off again to fly to England. At Selsey in Sussex she made a crash landing on the beach where she was rescued and taken in by some local people. The French authorities having applied for her extradition, I went down to Selsey, brought her to London, and eventually escorted her to France. She was tried for murder and found guilty but, such is the French attitude towards *crimes passionnel,* was freed. Later, she sometimes came to see me when she was in London. She was still flying and offered to take me up—an offer I thought best to refuse.

In 1938, I was a member of the so-called Murder Squad at Scotland Yard but, soon after the outbreak of war in 1939, I found myself in France once again. My visit this time resulted in the formation of a special unit in the British army to deal with the wholesale pilfering of stores and equipment. This unit was later to have its counterpart in the Royal Navy, the RAF, and the United States armed forces.

The word "pilfering," as familiar to every old soldier as the all-purpose euphemism "scrounge," is hardly adequate to explain the scale of operations in France at the beginning of the war. Advance units of the British Expeditionary Force landed there on September 9. From that moment on thousands of tons of stores of every description poured in. In the course of their being loaded and unloaded at ports, their transport to dumps and depots, and their subsequent distribution, thousands of men were involved. Those who were dishonest saw this as an open invitation to help themselves to anything they could lay hands on. And they accepted it. The professional thieves among them soon established contact with local receivers, and the French police, already overburdened with extra work created by the circumstances of war, had little time to spare for the affairs of their allies.

The situation became so serious and so widespread that three months after the BEF's arrival in France, the War Office asked for Scotland Yard's help in dealing with the matter, and I was told to go over and find out what was happening. At this stage however, no indication was given of the extent of the army's losses and from what little was said it sounded as though things were much as one would have expected them to be, with haphazard thefts of tinned meats, bacon, milk, cigarettes, and so on, from trains, sheds, and dumps where they had been unloaded en route to forward bases.

With such large numbers of men involved, I was prepared to find that the description given by the War Office of what was going on might well be an underestimate. I found that this was putting it mildly. From one ship alone, which had berthed at Brest, more than 24,000 cigarettes had been stolen, and from another, 14,000. Large quantities of food, chocolate, shaving cream, and other things had also been stolen from both ships. At Le Havre more than 26,000 razor blades (out of a total shipment of 50,000) had disappeared, along with nearly 1,400 articles of various kinds, including clothing, uniforms, cutlery, toothbrushes, etc. As might be expected, liquor was a favorite objective. Army vehicles, when they arrived from England, were found in some cases to have been stripped of all their accessories, spare parts, tools, and so on. It seemed that nothing was safe from the depredations of those who had found how much was to be made from these easy pickings.

At almost every port, railway siding, and depot I visited it was the same story. Vast quantities of all kinds of salable commodities were disappearing, often within hours of being landed. Helped by the blackout, by inadequate security precautions in buildings and compounds used for storage, and the fact that all units of the Provost Marshal's office and the Corps of Military Police were overworked and understaffed, thieves and black marketeers were reaping a tremendous harvest.

After making a tour of all the main points of entry and of distribution, and discussing the situation with the Sûreté in Paris and the British authorities at GHQ, I returned to London. As soon as I got back I prepared a report for the War Office on the measures that seemed to me necessary to put a stop to what was going on. It was obvious that arrangements for protecting stores at all stages of their journey from England to their eventual destination needed to be drastically overhauled, that many more guards would be required, and that an adequate and experienced force of police was needed to supplement these precautions. To these proposals the War Office reacted with surprising swiftness. Security arrangements were immediately tightened up everywhere and within a week five hundred policemen who had left their various forces to join the army were withdrawn from their units to form the nucleus of a preventive force. In a very short time they had the situation well under control. There was a rapid curtailment of the thieves' operations, followed by a corresponding depression in the black market.

In scope this inquiry was one of the most extensive I ever had to make. It was also one in which almost all the evidence was of negative value. There was merely the evidence of loss. It is always difficult to count the cost of crime, but I believe that the measures introduced in all three services, both in Britain and the United States, which followed this investigation, undoubtedly saved those services, not to mention the taxpayer, enormous sums of money.

Another proposal that I made was for the formation of a Special Investigations Branch staffed by CID officers from Scotland Yard. Little did I imagine the ultimate effects of this proposal. By the end of hostilities the SIB had extended its operations to every theater of war. It had investigated more than 22,000 cases, arrested over 38,000 soldiers and civilians, and recovered vast amounts of army stores looted in transit from docks and harbors to dumps and depots. In northwest Europe alone the value of property recovered amounted to £384,564.

The SIB's activities were by no means confined to cases of theft and operations on the black market. The arrest and conviction of Kramer, the so-called "Beast of Belsen," were largely due to SIB officers who were sent into various concentration camps to find witnesses and prepare statements about the atrocities committed in the camps.

In Alexandria a gang of thieves were found to be making a lucrative business of stealing trucks, driving them to the docks, and by means of forged passes, work tickets, and movement orders, loading them with army stores and taking them to Lebanon. Here the goods were sold with the connivance of a member of the Lebanese Chamber of Deputies and the proceeds invested in hashish, which was packed into four-gallon cans, sealed, and transported back to Egypt, where it was sold at an enormous profit. When the thieves were eventually arrested they were occupying a magnificent villa at Sidi Bishr and were running three large cars.

The activities of the SIB in India, where the territory of its operations was nineteen times the size of Britain, deserve special mention. In all, more than 3,000 people were arrested and as a result £786,500 worth of stolen property recovered. Attempted frauds in connection with the building of roads and bridges in Burma ended in the arrest of twenty-five civil contractors who had put in bogus claims to the Burmese government amounting to £27 million. Although on investigation these claims were disallowed, others had already been paid and of these £500,000 was eventually recovered.

Service with the Special Investigations Branch may not sound as risky as being in the front line, but in recognition of those who belonged to the SIB I should like to mention that in the course of duty 925 officers and men were killed or wounded and 935 cited for bravery in action.

To return briefly to the outline of my story, in 1943, I was appointed Detective Superintendent in charge of the CID in east and northeast London, and consequently found myself back once more in those regions of the East End where I had roamed as a boy and still felt quite at home. Three years later I was again transferred, this time back to Scotland Yard to take charge of the whole of the Detective Branch there. By 1951 the prospect of any further advancement seemed not very hopeful and after a while I began to think seriously of retiring and looking for something else to do, preferably a job less strenuous and with hours that were not quite so irregular. But having made this known, I was asked, somewhat to my surprise, if I would accept the rank of Deputy Commander of the Uniform Branch of the police when a vacancy occurred. After some consideration I accepted the offer, though as I pointed out, having spent almost the whole of my thirty-one years in the force in plain clothes engaged in detective work, I knew next to nothing about the duties of the Uniform Deparment which had changed drastically in all sorts of ways during the long interval since I had spent my two months on the beat. Although the ordinary police constable's responsibilities were fundamentally unchanged, his primary duties being those of protecting and assisting the public, the resources at his disposal were now far greater. Short-wave transmitters, mobile police in cars and on motorcycles, direct telephone and automatic alarm systems, and various other aids to law and order were now available. The speed and means of communication had vastly improved too and, as a result of this greater complexity of operational methods, so had the intelligence and training of the man on the beat. So for the first three months after I took over, I spent most of my time studying the Instructions Book used in basic training and finding out what exactly the uniformed policeman had to do.

The area of which I now became second-in-command, known as No. 1 District, extended from Westminster to well beyond London Airport, a sizable slice of the capital, and included the Houses of Parliament, all the main government buildings, the Royal Palaces, Westminster Abbey, and a number of other important places.

The duties of the Uniform Branch are many and various. Among them are arrangements for the conduct of State functions and the supervision of public demonstrations, of both of which I had my fair share. I had hardly settled into the job when King George VI died. His funeral provided me with my first experience of the skill in planning and the flexibility in operation of the Uniform Branch. The king's funeral was followed by arrangements for the coronation of the queen. Apart from war, this was perhaps the greatest test of organizational skill and resources that the Metropolitan Police have ever had to face in modern times.

Public demonstrations in my days with the Uniform Branch were confined largely to people with political grievances. Students were content for the most part to work hard for their degrees, and having been awarded them, became responsible and helpful members of the community. They did not spend their working hours in protest against the administration of their institutions and it was seldom, if ever, that the police were called to restore order at student meetings. I am not suggesting that student unrest is a phenomenon to be dismissed lightly. I can only say that I am thankful that while I was concerned with the Uniform Branch its members were spared the invidious and humiliating responsibilities forced upon them by a militant minority that seems to have less interest in acquiring knowledge and experience than in acquiring some undefined form of power.

Having been appointed Deputy Commander of the Branch at the age of fifty-six on February 2, 1952, it seemed unlikely that life in the force would have much more to offer. Nevertheless, two years later, on February 2, 1954, thirty-four years to the day since I had been sworn in as a police constable, I was asked by the Commissioner, Sir John Nott-Bower, to revert to my first love, the CID, and become its Commander. It was not in precisely those words that he offered me the post, but they are more or less in accordance with my feelings at the time.

The two years I spent with the Uniform Branch had given me a chance to reflect on various shortcomings in the CID in a way that I had never been able to while I was at the center of its operations and under the continual pressure of day-to-day events. One thing was clear to see. The modern criminal, in the methods and techniques that he used, was a far more intelligent crook than any with whom the police had had to deal in earlier days, and unless an equally intelligent approach were made to dealing with his activities, the crime rate would obviously continue to rise. Up to the time I took command there had been no specialist sections in the CID, such as I had seen in various countries abroad where detectives were trained specifically to investigate certain types of crime—murder, arson, forgery, fraud, and so on. During the next ten years various proposals that I made were put into practice, with the result that by the end of that time the strength of the CID had been more than doubled; the Flying Squad had been formed into a separate unit under its own chief and its numbers increased from fifty to a hundred men; both the Fraud Squad and the Provincial Crime Squad had been enlarged; two new sections had been formed, one to deal with the theft of cars (its activities, incidentally, were soon so successful that its size had to be increased); the other, the Intelligence Section, whose members specialized in gathering information about the activities of certain criminals regarded as potentially dangerous, who their associates were, their habits and spheres of operation, and their plans for future exploits. (In the sixties, before I left the Yard, yet another specialist squad was formed, the Drug Squad, which also had to be enlarged later on because of its ever-increasing activities.)

Another important operational change with which I was concerned was the breaking down of administrative boundaries between the Metropolitan Police and the forces of adjoining counties and the merging of their members in regional crime squads. All too often in the past, the activities of Scotland Yard and of police forces in the home counties had been hampered by mutual restrictions on their movements into each other's territories.

All these developments were put into effect after discussion with one of the ablest and most progressive Commissioners the Metropolitan Police had ever had, Sir Joseph Simpson. Another matter in which I took a very close interest was the reorganization and expansion of the Detective Training School in properly equipped premises in central London—hitherto training had been carried on in a large wooden hut at Hendon —and the expansion and revision of the syllabus to bring it up to date. In due course the staff was increased, refresher courses were introduced, and exhibits provided, so that there could be practical as well as theoretical training.

I have no doubt that all of these reforms would eventually have been brought about under the challenge of increasing crime. But that they occurred when they did seems paradoxically due to my having left the CID for the Uniform Branch. It was really this that gave me the opportunity to take a long, objective look at the way the CID was functioning. At the risk of sounding a note of complacency, the reforms within the CID that took place while I was in command seem to me probably the most useful contribution that I was able to make to the Yard's activities in the forty-five years that I spent there.

In July 1963, having reached the age of sixty-five, I was due to retire, but at Sir Joseph Simpson's suggestion I agreed to stay on for another year, so as to be able to see the effects of

[16]

the various changes that had been initiated. I accepted, thinking that I should be able to start taking things a bit easier. After so many years with the CID I should have known better. Eight days after my sixty-fifth birthday the Great Train Robbery took place. I decided, as soon as the Yard was called upon by the Buckinghamshire police, to take charge of the investigation myself. But that is another story—which is told later on.

I did not actually retire until September 30, 1964, and far from fading gradually from the scene, as I had hopefully supposed, on that day I was in the witness box until five in the afternoon, giving evidence at a court of inquiry appointed by the Home Office.

It would have been strange if after nearly forty-five years of police work I had not felt a little apprehensive about how I should settle down in retirement; whether after so long a time spent always on call, I should not begin to feel restless and frustrated by a life devoid of unforeseen troubles. It did not take me long to discover that my fears were unjustified. At last there was time to do many things I had often wanted to do, but had never had time for: to read books of my own choice instead of endlessly studying files, reports, and long-winded statements; to travel for my own enjoyment instead of in answer to an urgent summons from some foreign or provincial police force; to visit the many friends I had made abroad, not to discuss crises, but to enjoy holidays with them and wander round their countries. And last but by no means least, to wander about the English countryside at my leisure, which I had had virtually no chance to do since those days when I had explored it from London on my bicycle. These new explorations have taken me in many directions and have enabled me to see the great cathedrals, churches, castles, and country houses that have played so famous a part in the long history of England. Far from the days seeming too long, I still find that they seem much too short.

Detective
Training

(2)

☞ I have sometimes heard it said that a good detective is
born, not made. Personally, I don't agree with this, though it
is true that a detective needs certain qualities of character and
a view of human nature that are not common to everyone. In
talking to students at the end of their courses at the Detective
Training School I used to stress the importance of these factors. A detective's success, for instance, will depend largely on
the extent to which he is prepared to sacrifice things that men
in other occupations look on as part of their ordinary existence
—some regularity in their hours and conditions of work; a job
that is without the inconvenience, unpleasantness or even
danger that are often the hazards of a criminal investigation;
and last but by no means least, the comforts of home. I sometimes used to advise young detectives in training to have some
photographs taken which they could give to their families to
remind them of what they looked like, because frankly, the

chances of a dedicated detective leading a normal domestic life are *nil*.

There is no glamour in crime. Most of it is sordid and in many cases it is vicious, brutal, or even bestial. Those who commit petty crimes such as stealing, breaking and entering, and so on, are often too lazy to work or think themselves clever enough to be able to make a living out of crime. Some, on the other hand, are of low intelligence. In carefully contrived and systematic frauds those concerned are, of course, of quite a different class. Nevertheless, their motives can be accounted for only by greed.

The detective's view of human nature, biased as it must be by continual contact with crime, must nevertheless be neither indifferent, nor too sympathetic—criminals are often very good at eliciting sympathy when it is least deserved. The detective's view, therefore, must be as balanced and objective as possible at all times, which is considerably more often than most people are balanced or objective in their conduct.

Obviously a detective needs to keep himself physically fit, and he must also keep his natural faculties well up to scratch. One of the most important of these is curiosity, because curiosity leads to knowledge and the more a detective knows, the greater his advantage over the criminal, for by and large, it is the more ignorant type of person who turns to crime. He should want to know, of his own accord, as much as his job, or his leisure, if he has any, will allow him to learn. If he has to handle a case concerning some unusual subject, he will be at a disadvantage if he shows that he knows nothing whatever about it. So he needs not only to study; he must take every chance that comes his way to learn and especially to read about things unconnected with his work and to absorb all he can from the people he meets or has to deal with. An antique dealer will provide a chance for him to learn about old furniture, pictures, and so on; a jeweler will talk about gem settings, the cutting of various kinds of precious stones, or gold and silver hallmarks; chemists will talk about poisons and other substances; accountants about accountancy; booksellers will talk about books, printers about printing. From every craftsman, tradesman, or professional man there is something to be learned that may turn out one day to be useful. For instance, as I well know, knowledge of the Continent and of how one travels about, and of the various formalities that are necessary in different countries, may save days or even weeks of work. A knowledge of local habits and customs, and of food, drinks, and so on may do the same.

Next to developing a sense of curiosity I should place patience and an even temper as among the most valuable qualities in a detective. Many a time have I knocked at a door to find out about somebody from his neighbors and been met by a flood of gossip from the lady of the house. But if you interrupt a garrulous person you may well shut him or her up for good. If you have the patience to listen, often out of the flood will come a particular bit of information that will give you just the lead you have been looking for. On the other hand, if someone has seen or experienced something extraordinary or sensational, they are often apt to embroider their account of what happened, and allowance must be made for this.

Qualities akin to patience are tact and politeness. To show impatience is invariably tactless; in a detective it can be a fatal flaw; so can officiousness. The way in which he interviews someone can make all the difference between that person being cooperative or being hostile or shy or evasive. In most investigations you come across someone whose feelings have been ruffled, if not outraged. A brusque or tactless comment can only make matters worse; indignation often turns to incoherence and anxiety to alarm or hysteria.

Another faculty of vital importance is observation. Some people are naturally more observant than others. I have found this particularly true of children, who will often notice details about such things as cars, clothes, or other things they are interested in, which adults will often forget or overlook.

Finally, there is the faculty of persistence, without which a detective will never make headway. Routine procedures of detection often become appallingly monotonous, the endless telephone calls, the comparison of statements one with another, the house-to-house inquiries—however tedious, these things have to be done. Few people realize what house-to-house inquiries involve or appreciate the deadly monotony of them. Yet everything may depend on persistent questioning by the officers involved. More often than not this is a thankless task. Usually it means disturbing people at inconvenient moments—mothers preparing meals for clamoring children, women in the middle of their domestic chores, or someone watching his favorite TV program. Not unnaturally, such intrusions are sometimes resented and the officer has to use all his tact and powers of persuasion to get the person he is interviewing to cooperate. At the end of the day, after going from house to house through street after street, perhaps armed with a long questionnaire and asking the same set of questions over and over again, it would hardly be surprising if a detective did not feel strained and exhausted. Yet no matter what his reception, he must always remember to show courtesy and forbearance. A good detective never lets up, no matter how long an inquiry may last or a suspect have to be watched. It was four years before Chief Superintendent Butler arrested Bruce Reynolds for his part in the Great Train Robbery. And it was not just a coincidence that he was eventually found in his Torquay hideout. It was largely through Butler's persistence in following every thread, every piece of information, however insubstantial, that seemed to offer a possible clue to Reynold's whereabouts.

What I may call long-term investigation and detection, such as was involved in the capture of Bruce Reynolds, is not as exciting or spectacular as some of Sherlock Holmes's exploits and those of some other fictional detectives, and so it seldom makes the headlines until the denouement is achieved. What fascinated Conan Doyle's readers was Holmes's deductive method, based as it was—a novelty in those days—largely on scientific or technical data. Even so, some of his cases seemed too fantastic to be credible, but today, the part that science plays in the investigation of crime has outstripped even the most fanciful ideas of detective-story writers. Nevertheless, as

I have already indicated, the scientist alone cannot solve a crime, though science will play an ever-increasing part in criminal investigations.

The scientist working at the scene of a crime may find and examine blood, dust, dirt, or other clues, but it is the investigating officer who has to find the suspect. If traces of what the scientist has found are discovered on the suspect's clothes or person and correlate with one another, this will provide good circumstantial evidence, but is not a proof of guilt. The detective must learn to take every possible advantage of the help science affords, just as he must learn other elements of his craft which have little to do with the faculties I have just mentioned, which are either innate or can be enhanced by practice.

For example, detectives must learn early on that nothing should be touched at the scene of a crime and that it is just as important not to leave anything about that was not there before their arrival. A detective investigating a crime indoors should never smoke. Not only may the smell of tobacco obliterate other smells, but burned matches or cigarette butts may lead the detective in charge to suppose they have some relevance to the crime and cause him to jump to conclusions. To do so is, for a detective, a crime in itself. In every case it is vital to fit your theory, if you have one, to the facts, not the facts to your theory. And facts are no use unless they have been carefully and critically observed. Fragmentary clues, such as a shred of cloth, charred paper, or a few grains of sand or sawdust on the floor, may turn out to be of the utmost importance in the later stages of an investigation, provided that their exact position or dispersal have been accurately observed and recorded. Measurements, of course, must always be precise and never guessed at, and written notes should be taken about anything that looks as though it may be of significance. As the investigation gets under way and more and more facts are brought to light, the significance of various details—like a jigsaw puzzle that has been stared at too long—sometimes becomes more and more puzzling. But if at this stage the detective refers back to the notes he made at the beginning about what he has observed, he may see things in a very different light. The pieces of the puzzle will fall into place and the facts into perspective.

Detectives must learn, too, the importance of assuring that witnesses in a trial present down-to-earth evidence which will be easy for the average man or woman on a jury to appreciate. Experts called by the prosecution may have their evidence refuted by defense experts, and the conflicting opinions on matters beyond their understanding may result in jurors ignoring the controversy entirely.

When I went to the Criminal Investigation Department in 1920, we had a five weeks' training course in criminal law and procedure which occupied two hours of each working afternoon and was followed by an examination. Homework had to be done in what was euphemistically called our spare time. As our working day was generally from about 9:00 A.M. to 10:00 P.M. or even later, weekends included, this meant not only burning the midnight oil, but sometimes getting up before dawn to read, and going on reading as we went about on buses, trams, or trains. Nothing was mentioned in the course about forensic medicine, scientific aids, ballistics, firearms, foot- or fingerprints, or the many other subjects that are dealt with nowadays at the Detective Training School. The young detective in those days acquired most of his knowledge in the hard school of experience. He was taken as a "dogsbody" by senior detectives on important cases and learned his craft in a practical way. Much, too, was learned by trial and error. There was no Police Laboratory as we know it today, and if a detective had to deal with bloodstained clothing or instruments, he had to decide for himself what value they might have as evidence. If he wanted an expert's opinion in a murder case, he generally went to a hospital pathologist. If a body was exhumed, the officer himself had to arrange for the various organs to be removed and would usually have to put them in ordinary bottling jars to take them away for examination. According to the nature of the case, he would collect dust, fibers, paper, food, refuse, and so on, pack such substances in whatever was handy, and take them to a manufacturer for technical or scientific advice. Nowadays he is able to call on the services of all sorts of experts whose analyses, experiments, and opinions are often invaluable. But no amount of technical or scientific expertise is of any use by itself. It is the trained intelligence, the imagination and the experience of the man on the spot, the officer in charge of the case, that tells in the long run for the simple reason that whatever decisions are to be made must be made by him. If the decision he makes is wrong, his reputation may not be the only thing to suffer. The safety and security of the public may be involved too—a consideration he must never allow himself to forget.

In the early 1930s the Metropolitan Police Laboratory was founded, and at the same time the Detective Training School, where proper courses are now held and trainees are taught not only criminal law and procedure—and much more thoroughly than in my early days—but also—and this list is by no means exhaustive—about criminal investigation, Judges' Rules (on the interrogation and the taking of statements), the rules of evidence, powers of arrest and interrogation, fingerprints, photography, accountancy (with relevance to commercial fraud), company law, falsification of accounts, and banking. There are also lectures by experts in such things as police communications, Interpol, extradition procedures, drugs, poisons, ballistics, firearms, explosives, precious metals, gems, forensic medicine, antiques, motor cars, the work of the Customs and Excise department, and the Transport and Port of London Police, and the Borstal and prison systems.

The course is intensive and lasts ten weeks. At the end of it there is an examination to decide whether the candidate shall be posted permanently to the Criminal Investigation Department. If he passes—and he will need 75 percent of the possible total of marks in order to do so—he will have to go from time to time on refresher courses which deal with new legislation, new applications of forensic science, and the ever-developing techniques, scientific and operational, adopted by criminals.

So far I have spoken only about *men* as detectives, simply because there are far more of them than there are women detectives. But the part that women play in the operations of the CID in the Metropolitan and other police forces is often of the greatest value and importance.

The idea that policewomen belong to a race apart, that they are mostly grim-faced females of masculine aspect (which in the early days may have had something to do with their rather unbecoming uniforms), never had much foundation and nowadays has none whatever. In fact, such an appearance would be a handicap. The more informal and attractive a CID girl looks, the better her chances of mixing easily in a crowd or establishing friendly relations with a suspect. In certain situations a girl may have an advantage over a male detective, whose mere physical presence might in such circumstances arouse suspicion. But I would defy anyone to pick out a woman CID officer on duty, whether shopping in a supermarket, drinking with friends in a pub, or lunching at a West End restaurant.

When women were first attached to the Metropolitan police in 1919, two out of a total of 100 were appointed to help the CID, their sole duties being to take statements from women and girls involved in sexual cases. By degrees, as the value of their initiative and potential as detectives came to be better appreciated, their number was increased. Now, in the Metropolitan police alone, there are more than 100 women of various ranks in the CID engaged not only in sexual cases but in dealing with crimes of all sorts. In every respect these women are trained and treated in exactly the same way as the men of the CID. They share with them the same responsibilities and the same risks, which all of them accept with the same stoicism and courage. It can be no joke to act as a decoy on a dark night in an area where attacks have persistently been made on solitary women. Yet on a number of occasions CID girls have willingly done this and as a result dangerous thugs have been caught and convicted. In one of the first cases of this kind Detective Sergeant Watts was attacked and injured. She was the first woman police officer to be awarded the King's Police Medal for gallantry.

Another example of how tough and how resourceful a woman detective needs to be comes to mind with the case of

William Purdey. In 1953, Purdey, who was suspected of belonging to a gang of dangerous criminals, was found to be living in a chalet near a caravan site in Surrey. In order to keep him under observation, two young women detectives, Edna Slack and Daphne Skillern, were installed in one of the caravans from which the chalet could be clearly seen. The girls' cover story was that they were nurses who had had a long spell of looking after a private case and were now taking a rest. It could hardly have been called a holiday. It was the depths of winter, sometimes raining, sometimes snowing, bitterly cold and water had to be drawn and carried by bucket from a standpipe which was occasionally frozen.

The girls' Flying Squad contact visited them disguised as a farm laborer and sometimes went eavesdropping with them at night to find out what Purdey was up to. Two men who visited him regularly were identified from the girls' descriptions of them as Geoffrey Joseph and Ernest Robinson, both wanted by the police. A touch of irony was added to the situation one evening. In pouring rain one of the girls left the caravan to walk a mile and a half to a telephone box in order to report the men's arrival at the chalet. On the way, she was overtaken by Robinson in his car, who insisted on giving her a lift.

In the early hours of a March morning, shortly after a mail van had been robbed by a gang using two cars, the girls saw two cars without lights arrive at the chalet. One of the girls immediately contacted the Flying Squad, the chalet was surrounded and Purdey was arrested. In the expectation that one of the other men might return, some officers stayed behind. Joseph did indeed show up, but made off in a stolen car before they could catch him. A more cautious criminal, or one less scared, would hardly have taken such an obvious step as to rush straight to Robinson, as Joseph did, for the police, having themselves located Robinson beforehand, were able to arrest them both.

Robinson died in prison while awaiting trial, but Purdey and Joseph, for their various offences, were each sentenced to fourteen years' preventive detention.

The prolonged and acute discomfort and the very real danger to which Edna Slack and Daphne Skillern submitted themselves—discovery of their activities by any of the gang might well have had appalling consequences—were remarked on by the judge at the trial and both girls were specially commended by the Commissioner.

When all is said and done, the human element is still the most vital in the investigation of crime. The officer in charge of the case has to assume complete control of everything connected with the investigation—the collecting of clues and information, the preservation of vital data, the interrogation of witnesses, the checking of statements and records, the briefing of experts, and so on. Finally, after considering all the evidence, he has to decide whether he is satisfied beyond reasonable doubt that the case is sufficiently strong for him to charge the suspected person with committing the crime. When it is considered what is often at stake, the seriousness of this responsibility becomes obvious. A man's liberty, livelihood, and reputation may be destroyed. Large sums of public money may be spent and the time of the courts heavily committed, as well as that of the jury, witnesses, and counsel. It is not a responsibility to be taken lightly.

If the officer decides to bring a charge, at this point he will have to prepare a full report on the circumstances of the crime and the evidence he has obtained to support the prosecution. In a case of murder, apart from evidence that may be forthcoming from witnesses, there will be that of the police surgeon and perhaps other doctors; the findings of the postmortem; evidence about blood groups; and if a weapon has been used, the results of laboratory examination of it, and possibly of other clues. The officer will also have had photographs taken and plans made of the scene of the crime and will have listed in detail the exhibits that will be produced in court, for the safe custody of which he is at all times responsible. Finally, copies of all documentary material have to be made for the judge, the jury, and defending counsel. All this often involves an immense amount of meticulous work, but when it has been done the prosecution will have a complete picture of the circumstances of the case.

Every detective experiences from time to time the bitterness of frustration. Sometimes crimes such as robbery with violence, in which someone is seriously injured, or even murder, are committed by criminals whose identity is known beyond all reasonable doubt but against whom there is no *legal* proof. The officer concerned may spend weeks, or even months, trying to gather enough evidence to justify the criminal being charged, but without success. After every possible line of inquiry has been explored, all that happens is that the officer, to his mortification, sees the criminal not only go scot free, but often enjoying the proceeds of his crime. What adds to the officer's sense of frustration is that in such cases the public inevitably regards the case as unsolved and consequently thinks the police have been less assiduous or efficient than they might have been. In such cases the officer's long-term hope must be that the criminal, as happens surprisingly often, will eventually be caught and convicted for another offense.

Then there are those cases in which a jury considers the evidence insufficient to justify a verdict of guilty. There have been murder cases, women usually being the victims, in which the accused man has been acquitted, the jury being unaware, because of the rules of evidence, that he has previously been acquitted of a similar type of murder, and he has then committed what the police well know to be his third murder.

I have spoken of some of the qualities it takes to make a good detective. There are, of course, a number of others, but those I have mentioned—curiosity, patience, tact, observation and persistence, are certainly among the most valuable. It may be of some interest to mention briefly a few cases which illustrate in their various ways the importance of these particular qualities.

It was due to curiosity—about the habits and customs of people abroad—that I was able on one occasion to help the Belgian police. Two women who had poisoned themselves were found dead in a Brussels hotel, where they had registered as British subjects. Every mark of identification had been removed from their clothing and luggage, but in their room were some English bank notes and newspapers. I was stationed in Brussels at the time and the police asked me to have a look at the women to see if I could make any suggestions about their identity. In going through their belongings I noticed that they had even scratched the maker's name off their shoes; an unnecessary precaution, it seemed to me, because if they had come from a city as big as London or Birmingham, the possibility of tracing the shop where they had been bought would have been out of the question. I next had a look at their luggage and in one trunk I found a lot of bed linen. It was not folded as English housewives fold their sheets, but lengthwise and was made up into neat rolls. Now I happened to know that this is the way Scandinavian women fold their bed linen. I suggested making inquiries first of the Swedish police, with the result that the women were very soon identified as having come from Helsingfors, and consequently a considerable amount of time and trouble was saved.

When it comes to patience the police usually have an advantage. The detective can often afford to play a waiting game; not so the criminal. Patience, allied with a knowledge of local habits and customs, played its part when on Christmas Day, 1944, the body of a girl, partially burned, was found on a bed in a flat at Dagenham in Essex, the flat having been obviously set on fire in several places. The girl's body was removed to the mortuary for a postmortem and meanwhile I had inquiries made to discover who her men friends were. At the same time I gave instructions that none of them was to be contacted. The postmortem, which ended at noon, showed that the girl had been strangled, and also that she was more than two months pregnant. Dagenham being a working-class district, I took it for granted that the menfolk would be in the pubs until they closed at 2 P.M. while the women were getting their Christmas dinners ready. I therefore gave my men orders to go out at about three o'clock and fetch in the men whom the girl had known. I told them they were not to say anything at all to these men, except that I wanted to see them at the police station. I was curious to see how they would behave. I then went out and had a few sandwiches and came back to the station at about a quarter-past three. Several young men had been brought in and all but one were fairly threatening to pull the station down. As I had anticipated, they were in the middle of their Christmas dinners and were furious at having been taken away from them without being told why. The odd man out was half-way through his dinner when my men had called. When he was asked to go with them he simply said, "All right," then got up and put his jacket on. He asked no questions and raised no difficulties; it was obvious that he was expecting a visit from the police. I apologized to the other men and let them go. Before long, under interrogation, the young man whom we had detained confessed to killing the girl because she had been pestering him to marry her.

The rewards of tact are shown, somewhat ironically, by a case that occurred in 1939, when I was in charge of the CID in the West End. A smash-and-grab raid occurred in Charlotte Street, near Soho. A man smashed the window of a jeweler's shop, grabbed a tray of rings worth £4,000, and got away in a car driven by a man who had red hair. Later we found that the car, which had been in a collision and then abandoned, belonged to a car-hire firm, but needless to say, the man who had hired it had given a false name and address. All we had to go on was a rather sketchy description of him by people who had seen the snatch; he was said to be between twenty-six and twenty-eight years old, about five feet eight inches tall, clean-shaven, and dark. A more promising detail which we got from the car-hire firm was that he wrote with his left hand. At the Yard we turned up the index of left-handed men between the ages of twenty-five and thirty and of the same physical description as the robber. There were about eighty that seemed to fit the bill. We next took from the files samples of their handwriting and signatures which we compared with the writing on the car-hire firm's document and finally decided that the writing on it coincided with that of a man whose record we had. So we made inquiries about him and found he was missing, which was a good sign.

The routine, in looking for someone who is missing, is to find out who his or her associates are, and particularly whether they have any girlfriends. The criminal who works alone gets much farther than the one who ties himself up with a woman. We found this man's girlfriend and went to see her. She professed to know nothing whatever about him and denied that she even knew him. I noticed that she was pregnant and took a chance on the possibility that he intended making an "honest woman" of her; inquiries were made at churches and registry offices in the area and I found that at one of these notice of marriage had been given by the man we were looking for. I waited for the wedding day and when the bride and bridegroom turned up, I was there to welcome them. I had a talk with the bridegroom, told him I intended to arrest him, and asked him what he would like to do—be married first and then come to the police station, or vice versa. After talking things over with the bride, the two of them decided to get married first. I said that in that case I would have to remain as an uninvited guest.

While I was talking to the bridegroom the best man arrived. I was pleased to notice that he had red hair, and after the ceremony I told him I intended to take him to the police station too. And then the whole party, parents and friends, asked if they could come as well. I said "Certainly." At the station we had to arrange for an identification parade; meanwhile the whole party sat in my office. The parade took some time to organize and I was asked if they could have a drink in the meantime to celebrate. I had no objection, provided they paid for what they wanted, so they asked that a bottle of whisky should be sent for.

When the parade was ready I went back to my office and found them all sitting round the table with the whisky poured out, but untouched. I asked what they were waiting for. It turned out that they were waiting for me, so that I could propose a toast to the bride and bridegroom and their future happiness. This I did, though perhaps without much conviction. As I had guessed from the bridegroom's record, the honeymoon eventually had to be postponed for two years.

The importance of a detective's being observant needs no emphasis. However, it is surprising how unobservant most other people seem to be. Statements made by witnesses often show astonishing variation, only sometimes due to myopia; more often, I think, they are due to lack of curiosity, if not sometimes to the promptings of the imagination. In Mrs. Barney's trial for murder at the Old Bailey in 1932, a witness swore under oath that she had seen from a distance of several yards the smoke from a revolver fired out of a window. Unfortunately for her credibility, the next witness was able to prove that the ammunition that had been used was smokeless. Sometimes other factors may affect what a witness says. I once instructed an officer to keep observation on a house where a woman suspect wearing a red coat was expected to call during the evening. The officer later reported that although another woman had arrived at the house, the suspect had not turned up. Now I knew from other information that she had called. I also knew the officer to be completely reliable. I later discovered the discrepancy was due to fluorescent lighting in the street under which the woman's red coat had appeared to be greeny-gray.

Sherlock Holmes's powers of observation may perhaps strike the ordinary reader as rather exaggerated, but in my experience nothing that he spotted during his many investigations would be likely to have gone unnoticed by a well-trained detective. An instance of this occurred in 1944, when the rockets were falling on London. One came down near an office where I was working and killed some forty people. After the dead and wounded had been removed I went to the local police station to find out the number of casualties. While I was there a policeman came in to report the finding of another body which had been taken to the mortuary. It was that of a young woman who had apparently died of shock. The policeman said he had been called to a house by a woman who said that some time after the raid three girls, one of them very much shaken up, had knocked at her door and asked if they could come in and sit down. The girl who was in a bad way seemed on the point of collapse, so the woman had given her some whisky and

called a doctor, but by the time he arrived the girl was dead. I
was a bit puzzled by this. It was an hour and a half since the
rocket had fallen, which seemed to me rather a long time, if
the girl's death were due to delayed shock. Postmortems were
not held on air-raid victims; there were far too many, so after
identification their bodies were handed over to their relatives
for burial. Not being entirely satisfied with what I had heard, I
went along to have a look at the girl in the mortuary. They had
just taken off her dress and slip and I noticed that her under-
pants had been put on inside out and back to front. I thought
this was odd, so I stopped things going any further and rang up
the coroner and asked if he would arrange for a postmortem
examination. This was carried out and it was found that she
had indeed died of shock—but not as a result of the raid: she
had died as the result of an air embolism following an abortion. The discovery of this led, after various inquiries, to the
arrest and eventual conviction of a woman living at the house
where the girl had died, who was active as an abortionist
among girls working in factories.

I have mentioned the need for persistence in a detective. Its
value was seldom more evident than during the inquiry into
the Potters Bar golf course murder on April 29, 1955. The dead
body of a woman was found on the seventeenth green after she
had failed to return home from an evening walk with her dog.
She had been partially strangled with a nylon stocking and
beaten about the head with the iron green-marker. There was
some evidence to suggest that the murderer had started to
molest her sexually. This type of murder almost always pre-
sents problems. Such crimes are seldom committed by anyone
known to the police. They are usually committed by apparently
quite ordinary people who have always kept out of trouble,
so that two obvious sources of inquiry, the Criminal Record
Office, and that unattractive but useful character, the nark or
police informant, are ruled out. And so it appeared in this case.
All that we had to go on was a palm print found on the green-
marker. We drew a blank after comparing it with the small
number of recorded palm prints in the Criminal Record Office
files. Meanwhile, a number of provincial police forces were

asked to establish the whereabouts on the night in question of
certain men with records of sexual violence and to take their
palm prints. These were men who were known either to have
escaped from mental institutions or to have been in the Potters
Bar area on the night of the murder. As a result, inquiries were
made in thirty-one counties and twelve cities and boroughs
in the United Kingdom, as well as by the Dublin Civic Guard,
the Provost-Marshal of the British forces in West Germany,
and the police in California, Canada, Australia, Eritrea, and
the Gold Coast. Again we drew a blank.

Investigation of a crime of this kind invariably involves an
enormous number of house-to-house inquiries, in this case
more than 7,000. In addition, all the local factories were visited
and palm prints taken of every worker, numbering some 2,000
in all.

By the middle of June, as we were no nearer to a solution, I
gave authority for palm prints to be taken from every willing
male member of the population of Potters Bar. Twelve men in
the Yard's Fingerprint Department were taken off all other
duties to cope with the huge task of comparing the results with
prints in the files, a tricky and delicate job. By August 19,
8,889 prints had been taken and 4,604 examined. At that point
we did not need to examine any more: we had found what we
wanted—a print which belonged to a local youth identical
with that on the green-marker. He was seen by the police and
confessed to the murder, for which at his trial he was ordered
to be *detained during Her Majesty's pleasure* (the law's way of
saying that the case will be reviewed periodically with a view
to deciding whether the offender's imprisonment should continue. The date was October 12, nearly six and a half months
after the murder. Such clues as there were, apart from the
palm-print, had yielded nothing, nor had the thousands of inquiries that had been made. It was simply and solely through
the persistence of all those concerned in the endless monotony
of the inquiry that the murderer was eventually discovered.

One thing I have not mentioned so far is the faculty of deduction, which in its simplest form really means no more than
using common sense. Applied to detection, however, it means

using it much more precisely than usual in relation to data or circumstances that are often out of the ordinary. It was a matter of fairly simple deduction that led to the solution of a crime that came to light in November 1945, with the discovery of a new-born baby's body which was washed up on the foreshore of the Thames at Greenwich. The postmortem examination showed the child to have been about two weeks old and that shortly before it died it had had a meal of Cow and Gate food. It was estimated that its body had been in the water for a week or more. Except for a piece of tape tied round the wrist, on which the words "Baby Clegg" were written in indelible ink, the child's body was naked. Such tapes are often used in lying-in hospitals and maternity wards to identify babies and without much difficulty we found that the child had been born on October 19 at St. Bartholomew's Hospital and that its mother's name was Joan Clegg. She was twenty and unmarried.

Her father, whom we interviewed in the course of the inquiry, said that he had met a woman called Mrs. Clarke in a pub at Loughton—some considerable way from where he lived in Lambeth—who had agreed to adopt the child, and that on October 30, after it had been given some Cow and Gate food, he had met Mrs. Clarke in the pub again and handed the baby over. He did not know where Mrs. Clarke lived and could only give a vague description of her. It was not a very convincing story and I decided to try and test it. I found first of all that no one at the pub had any recollection of seeing Clegg or Mrs. Clarke. I also found out that Clegg's job necessitated his traveling about in a hired car which he paid for according to the length of each trip. This meant, of course, that the firm from which he hired the car checked the speedometer before and after each of his journeys. Clegg was asked to give details of the route he had taken on October 30 and this he did. I then had exactly the same journey, ending at St. Bartholomew's Hospital, made by a police car. Deducting the mileage from that recorded by the car hire garage, there was a difference of about ten miles. Continuing the journey, from the hospital to Loughton and then back to the garage, accounted for another thirty miles. From the hospital to Greenwich and back to the garage was a distance of ten miles. I therefore asked Clegg to call and see me with a view to his explaining about the twenty miles not recorded on his speedometer, which would have shown if the journey to Loughton had been made. He was unable to do so and in view of this and the other circumstantial evidence that had been accumulated I decided to charge him with murder. Although he pleaded not guilty, he was eventually convicted, sentenced to death and hanged.

The value of scientific evidence given in support of good detective work was well demonstrated in a murder trial that took place in the summer of 1938. Early on a Sunday morning a young woman was found strangled in a country lane. She had been raped, and her cotton dress had been ripped from her body. The lane where she was found was little more than a sandy track and in the soft soil between her parted legs was the imprint of her attacker's knees, clearly showing the pattern of his trousers. A plaster cast was taken of the imprint.

During inquiries which followed, many men were interviewed. Among them was one who had known the dead girl slightly. He was not seen until three or four days after the inquiry had begun. It was then noticed that the pattern of his suit was different from that of the imprint found in the lane. Bearing in mind that the girl had been murdered on a Saturday evening, or possibly later, the officer in charge asked the young man to produce his "Sunday suit." When the pattern of it was compared with the plaster cast of the imprint seen on the ground, they were found to correspond. Though this was significant, it was not enough in itself to do more than increase the officer's suspicions. He therefore had a vacuum cleaner used on the trousers, with the result that some grains of sand were extracted, which scientific examination proved to be identical with the sandy soil in the lane. The vacuum cleaner also picked up a single thread of colored cotton. This was submitted to the manufacturers of the girl's dress, who were able to state positively that it was made of seven twisted threads, and in this respect, as well as in its color, was identical with the cotton from which the dress was made. No other evidence was forthcoming, but this was sufficient to justify the young man being charged. During the trial, in which he put forward an alibi, he elected to give evidence on his own behalf. However during his cross-examination he suddenly broke down and confessed to the murder, for which he was eventually hanged.

I should like to cite one final example to show how in a relatively simple case quick thinking may go a long way towards finding the solution. In this particular case my knowledge of traveling formalities was also useful.

During the summer of 1936, the German car magnate, von Opel, returned from a holiday to find that his butler, Schiffbauer by name, was missing. It was not until a day or so later, when von Opel opened his private safe, that he found some £75,000 worth of jewelry was missing too. Schiffbauer's description was immediately circulated throughout Europe by the German police, with the request that if he were found he should be arrested and held pending extradition.

In Britain every foreigner who enters the country has to fill in a card giving various details about himself and his British address. These cards are kept in the Home Office Traffic Index, so as soon as the cable came from the German police I went to have a look at the Index and there I found Schiffbauer's name. His address was given merely as "a hotel in London." This finished all hope of being able to trace him in the short time he intended to stay, as indicated by his card. The card showed also that he had come from Denmark, which gave me to wonder whether it was his intention to travel farther west, i.e., to the United States. Now, to enter America it is necessary to get a visa from the United States consulate and this usually takes a few days. It was obvious that Schiffbauer would not have waited to apply for one in Germany, but would have fled straight away. Nor would he have had time, according to the details on his card, to have got a visa in Denmark. I therefore asked the United States consulate to let me know if he should turn up there to ask for a visa, and I then went to Bow Street magistrates' court and applied for a provisional extradition warrant.

I had hardly got back to the Yard when a call came from the

consulate: Schiffbauer was at that moment applying for a visa. I got there in time to see him leave and after he had gone a little way I arrested him.

At Bow Street under interrogation he said he was staying at a hotel off the Strand and that the jewelry was in his suitcase. I went to the hotel and found most of it, as he had said; also an envelope containing some hundreds of pounds, the proceeds of selling part of his loot, which fortunately we were able to recover. I took all the stuff back to the Yard, turned it out of the suitcase onto my desk, and then put it into the Superintendent's safe. This I did in something of a hurry, as the Superintendent had to leave for an appointment, and I have to confess that I did not immediately check the jewelry against the list of what was missing. When I came to do so the next morning I found that four valuable pieces worth approximately £12,000 were not there. I was puzzled by this. I knew they could not have been sold in London without arousing suspicion. Then I noticed that in replacing Schiffbauer's belongings the night before I had left on my desk a round box of powder about two inches deep. I pushed a pencil down into the powder and found it went in only half an inch; it was an old smuggler's trick. Below a cardboard disc underneath the powder was the missing jewelry.

In each of the cases I have cited the solution was arrived at partly through the exercise of one or the other of those inborn faculties that I mentioned earlier. Invaluable though these faculties are, experience counts for no less, and, indeed, much that you need to know as a detective can only be acquired by experience.

Experience also counts for a lot in helping to get used to some of the more grim and gruesome aspects of criminal investigation. A mutilated body, a severed head or limb, or the body of someone who has been hanged or drowned, are not pleasant to look at: nor is it an agreeable task to take the fingerprints of a putrefying cadaver or attend an autopsy on the body of a child who has been raped and murdered: but after you have seen or experienced such things a dozen times or more you come to accept them as being all part of the day's work. Perhaps to anyone not used to seeing or handling such things, this may sound somewhat callous. But however squeamish you may feel to begin with—and it would be unnatural if you did not feel so at first—as a detective you cannot afford to let your judgment be swayed or your perspicacity impaired by the various unpleasant spectacles with which you are bound to be confronted from time to time. And it is this capacity to remain unflurried in one's behavior and objective in one's estimation of the facts that offers the surest hope of arriving at the truth.

Experience, as well as education in the art, also plays a large part in one of the most difficult of all jobs the detective does—interrogation.

No part of a detective's job calls for greater subtlety in dealing with individuals. An officer may be highly efficient in various branches of police work, but lacking in the gift of psychological understanding that is essential to the successful conduct of an interrogation. The manner and circumstances in which an accused person has been interrogated before being charged with a crime are points on which defending counsel invariably seize if either seems to offer a chance of discrediting the case for the prosecution. It is therefore of the utmost importance to ensure that, as far as possible, suspects or witnesses are protected from pressure or intimidation while making statements to the police. The officer in charge of a case will very often have to face searching cross-examination about the circumstances in which the accused has made a statement, and any hint of irregularity or attempted coercion will be exploited to the detriment of the prosecution's case. But so long as a statement has been obtained fairly and is admissible as evidence the officer need have nothing to fear. This point is aptly illustrated by a remark attributed to that most formidable of defense lawyers, Sir Edward Marshall Hall, when accepting a brief: "Never mind about the details—what did the bloody fool say to the police?" It is what the "fool" may have said under interrogation that will be most likely to tell against him at his trial.

Interrogation is not confined to witnesses or suspects. Other people who may be interrogated are informants (I do not mean informants employed by individual officers, but people who voluntarily make allegations of crime against others) and self-confessed criminals. In dealing with either of these types strict caution is necessary. Those who allege crimes against others sometimes do so without any justification, but make such claims out of spite or for emotional reasons, as when a girl who finds herself pregnant alleges that she was raped by the man responsible for her condition. Such stories may sound quite convincing, and indeed they are sometimes difficult to disprove; so difficult on occasions that only the investigating officers' skill and persistence have prevented an innocent person from being charged with the crime. Nor does everyone who confesses to a crime necessarily speak the truth. It is not unknown for people to claim, for reasons of perverted vanity or from other causes, to have committed offenses of which they are innocent.

In all forms of interrogation the first essentials are patience, politeness, and an open mind. To try to elicit a bias in answer to one's questions may lead to erroneous replies that will only complicate the picture. Hardly less important are the circumstances in which an interrogation is conducted. The best place is obviously a police station, where there need be no distractions or interruptions and documents or exhibits that one may want to refer to will be easily available. It is hopeless to question someone in surroundings that are noisy, dirty, or overcrowded. To interview a man or woman in a bug-ridden tenement room, with children running about, is as unfair to the person you are interviewing as to yourself. In such surroundings concentration and clarity of thought and speech are impossible.

Defending counsel sometimes protest that taking a suspect to a police station means that he has been detained or arrested. But a police station is not only a place where prisoners are taken; it is where all forms of police business are conducted, and with efficiency and dispatch.

The need for privacy and a calm atmosphere is particularly important when a sexual crime or sexual details may have to be discussed. On such an occasion, if a woman is involved, the investigating officer should never interview her by himself; another officer, preferably a woman, should always be present. Some women suspected of a crime, particularly if they feel themselves to be in a tight corner, will make outrageous allegations against the officer interrogating them if they feel that it may help them to escape from their predicament.

It is also advisable to remove anything from a desk or table at which the person who is being questioned is sitting and which might be used as a weapon. On more than one occasion I have had such things as inkpots and heavy rulers thrown at my head.

An experienced officer will try to keep the emotional temperature as low as possible. He will also have developed some understanding of psychology and be able to spot the approach most likely to succeed, as well as to judge whether he is being told the truth or not. Not everyone who tells a lie gives himself away by the same sort of tricks or reactions, such as blushing or failing to look at you. Some will not give themselves away at all. But except in such cases, a kind of sixth sense will often indicate whether the person you are questioning is telling the truth or not. This is difficult to explain, still more to account for, but the feeling is one that any police officer who is used to examining suspects or hostile witnesses will confirm.

The interviewing of a suspect is a challenge to the mind of the interrogator, who must be on the look-out for abnormalities of behavior or inconsistencies in what is said. As the suspect's mental processes are gradually revealed, the interrogator must decide whether such processes are compatible with the apparent motive for the crime. If, when the motive is unknown, the interrogator can fathom the suspect's thoughts, he may be able to discern his probable reactions to a set of known circumstances (i.e., those in which the crime has been committed) and thus conclude with reasonable certainty what the motive is likely to have been.

There are a number of things that must be borne in mind by an officer conducting an interrogation, such as the obvious need to remain patient and keep calm and to frame his questions objectively and not in such a way as to hint at possible answers. He must bear in mind throughout the interview that its purpose is not to establish whether a suspect is guilty, but simply and solely to get at the truth. If he is asked in the witness box, as he may well be, why he decided to interrogate the accused, his answer must be, "To find out the facts," not "To see if he had committed an offense." An astute counsel would have no difficulty in interpreting such an admission of suspicion into an indication of bias.

Before he starts to question a suspect, the officer should try to find out as much about him as possible—his family background, his occupation, his interests, his religion, and if he has a criminal record, what this consists of, and his *modus operandi.* A knowledge of such things, which the officer will naturally keep to himself, will give him a considerable advantage in knowing how to handle the interview.

The preliminary appraisal of a suspect is extremely important and may give some indication of whether or not he is the right man. For example, a period of silence at the beginning won't as a rule upset a guilty person, but a person who is innocent will often get flustered and show some resentment. From an offender with a bad record the officer usually meets with passive resistance; the ex-convict will have seen it all before and gives himself time to think over his answers. An innocent party will usually show mistrust, but not resistance; in fact, in his desire to be explicit and his eagerness to prove his innocence he will often come out with a flow of circumstantial details that have little to do with the crime.

The judgment of a suspect's character is not easy, particularly if he has something to hide. Observation of behavioral habits, of posture, gestures, facial expressions is helpful, but one should beware of placing too much reliance on such things. To the innocent especially, the very fact of being interviewed by a detective is an unnerving and uncomfortable experience and normal reactions are apt to be disguised or diminished by a feeling of apprehension. A person who is accustomed to the procedure will, unless provoked, usually try to look impassive or else to laugh the whole thing off.

When a suspect starts off by insisting that he has a cast-iron alibi one's suspicions are aroused at once. Most people retain only a very imperfect recollection of routine events that have happened three or four days earlier. Usually they are unable to describe such things in detail, sometimes even to remember the precise order in which they occurred. In this respect one day seems very much like another. A guilty party, however, will often be found to "remember" any number of trivial details about his daily routine, if they look like lending support to an alibi. The man who can tell you exactly how long he spent in doing some minor chore or in traveling between three or four different places, all fairly close together, is pretty certain to be lying.

Of course, in estimating such factors as time or distance there is always an element of guesswork. But there is, or should be, far less in what a suspect says about articles found on him or at his house or premises. Particularly important is what he may have to say about their origins, which may enable inquiries to be started in new and unsuspected directions. But the interrogator must beware of pressing such inquiries too hard; undue emphasis on an article or a document will show the suspect how much importance the police attach to it.

Some people, when it comes to making a confession, do so not because they believe themselves to be inescapably cornered, and hope that by confessing they may get off, but from a sense of pride or vanity, to show how tough they are in order to make an impression on their friends. Such characters are usually the talkative ones and therefore easier to deal with than more reticent or nervous suspects. All you have to do is be patient and let them go on talking; if they are, in fact, guilty, they will almost certainly say something eventually that leaves no doubt about the truth of their confession.

Whoever is being interviewed, the interrogator should use the same sort of language as the suspect, however crude or slangy. This indication of an understanding of the suspect's habits of speech and circumstances is much more likely to evoke a truthful reaction than an attitude of stern authority.

I have often been asked what value is to be attached to the

use of truth drugs or lie detectors, on which much reliance is placed by some police forces in the United States. I can only say that I never used either. Both seem to me to involve a considerable risk that statements secured under such conditions might, at least in a British court of law, very easily be rendered worthless by skillful cross-examination of the officer who allowed them to be used. I believe one should be extremely cautious about introducing mechanical aids of this sort, even though taking down everything in long-hand may prolong the suspect's ordeal. For one thing, there is the possibility of a mechanical defect developing which might not become apparent until after the statement has been made, making it necessary for it to be repeated and thus giving the suspect a chance to retract or explain away admissions which he realizes might be damaging to himself.

A confession must not be regarded as an end in itself. It must be carefully checked and rechecked against all the evidence. When statements are quoted during a trial—including anything to which the accused may have confessed—they should find their place in the complete story of what happened before, during, and after the crime. In other words, the confession should supplement the proof. Hence the importance of interrogation in establishing the validity of a confession.

Interrogation is a subject about which there is always something new to learn and it is thus impossible to lay down a code of rules that will cover all circumstances that may arise.

Foreign
Transactions

(3)

Most of the cases that took me abroad while I was with the CID were concerned either with smuggling or forgery. The first important case of this sort was one that occurred in 1934. If for no other reason, it will stay in my memory because of the situation in which I found myself at one point—being interrogated as I have so often had to interrogate other people.

The case arose from a type of crime that is not very common, though undoubtedly lucrative; that of using Health Insurance stamps twice over by the simple expedient of removing the cancellation marks. The penalty for this offense is severe and not many employers are foolish enough to commit it. An alternative, if more expensive, method of cheating the Ministry is to buy forged stamps, provided you know where to get them.

In April 1934 an informant came to Scotland Yard with a story about a gang of forgers in Warsaw who were producing thousands of British insurance stamps which were being sold in London. It so happened that I had dealt with this informant in Brussels and had found him reliable, so it was suggested that he should go to Warsaw and try to find out what was going on.

He was away for some little time and when he returned it was with the names and addresses of the gang, three of whom he said were soon coming to London. A watch was kept for them at Harwich, where they eventually arrived. Arrangements had been made with the customs authorities for them not to be held up and they were shadowed throughout their journey by train and taxi until they reached their hotel. There they were seen in their room by Scotland Yard officers, who examined their bags. Close inspection revealed that the bags had false bottoms and underneath were found forged insurance stamps to the value of £43,700. All three men were arrested and charged with possessing the stamps, and that night I set off for Warsaw.

As soon as I got there I went to see Dr. Nagler, the Chief of Police, who had some other officials with him, and told them all that our informant had told us—his information was in considerable detail—and urged that those concerned should be arrested before they got wind of the fact that their friends had been picked up in London. To my surprise, the officials' reaction was distinctly reserved. In fact, they seemed none too pleased to hear how much we knew about the racket. Far from showing any sense of urgency, they said it would be better to raid the forgers' place at midnight. I made it clear that I particularly wanted to be present, so as to see what else the raid might disclose besides British insurance stamps; our information was that U.S. dollar bills were also being forged, so it seemed that possibly British notes might be being printed as well.

We then went out to lunch. It was a prolonged meal and by the time we returned to police headquarters it was five-thirty. Soon after we got back I was told not only that the suspected forgers, thirteen in all, had been arrested, but that their premises had been raided, that they had been sealed under a magistrate's order, and that no one would be allowed to inspect the place except those appointed by the court to do so.

In spite of every effort to find out more about what had been discovered, I could get no more information. Indeed, it was politely suggested that I would do better to return to London, where any further information would be sent to me. However, I hung about for a couple of weeks, still trying to find out what was going on, and eventually one evening I was asked to go to police headquarters. Here, through an interpreter, I was interrogated by an examining magistrate on all that I knew about the case, everything I had to say being taken down in writing. Having had considerable experience of Continental police procedure, I assumed that the purpose of this was that my statement could be produced later on in the proceedings against the accused. But not at all. The interview developed into a searching inquiry into whether I was engaged in some sort of secret work. Again and again I was questioned about this. The fact that my passport, which I was asked to produce, had been issued by the British consulate in Brussels (where I had been living when it was issued) intensified the magistrate's obvious suspicions and I began to realize what it must feel like to be on the wrong side of the table. My interrogation lasted, with a short break for a cup of tea, from about seven in the evening until six o'clock the next morning; then, after my statement had been read over to me, I put my signature to it. I stayed on in Warsaw for a little while, but as it was clear that the authorities were going to divulge nothing, I eventually left, having spent a fruitless and frustrating month.

From conversations I had had with various people, I had gathered that forgery was not an uncommon crime in Poland and that measures for its suppression were pretty lax. From my own experience I could well believe this. Of those in the case who were brought before the court, I found eventually that five were ordered to be detained indefinitely, four held pending further investigations, and four others released. At the trial of the three men arrested in London, one was sentenced to four years' imprisonment and the others to two years each.

Although personally I considered this a not very satisfactory conclusion to the case, the authorities at Scotland Yard seemed to think otherwise. Soon after my return I was promoted to the rank of Detective Inspector and put in charge of the West End. However, in spite of this, it was not long before I found myself being sent abroad again, and as before, to investigate a case of forgery.

It is not unusual in investigating the activities of a professional criminal, whose friends or associates are also likely to operate on the wrong side of the law, to unearth information about something quite different from the matter in hand. An accidental occurrence of this sort, an operational bonus, as it were, resulting from inquiries on which I was engaged in 1933, had a strange and complex aftermath. Little did I think at the time that it would be twelve years before the final installment of this bonus would be paid.

The case I was helping to investigate was one of arson, which aroused a considerable amount of interest at the time. Arson is a fairly uncommon crime and is usually committed by someone who does it from a perverted sense of pleasure or excitement, or with the more rational though no less reprehensible motive of collecting insurance on the property that is destroyed. The case in question involved an assessor called Leopold Harris, who, with others, until they were caught, made a profitable business out of committing arson systematically, covering their tracks with an elaborate network of operations that took a long time to unravel. During the course of the inquiry, I interviewed a businessman in the city whose premises had been burned down and for whom Leopold Harris had acted as assessor and prepared insurance claims. However, it turned out that in this particular case there were no grounds for suspicion, so as far as the police were concerned that seemed to be the end of the matter. In fact, for me it was only the beginning of a case of a very different nature.

In October 1934, more than a year after the inquiries into Harris' affairs, I was again investigating a case in the city, and finding myself with a little time to spare, I decided to have a cup of coffee. I went into a teashop and sat down opposite a respectable-looking man of about sixty with whom I presently got into conversation. He was well dressed, quietly spoken, and from his conversation seemed to have traveled extensively throughout Europe. He gave me no clue as to what his occupation might have been and I thought he was probably a retired businessman. Just as I was about to leave I heard a voice behind me say, "Hullo, George," and thinking someone was speaking to me, I looked round. There I saw the man whom I had interviewed during the inquiry into the Harris case; but it was not me he was speaking to, it was the man sitting opposite. My city acquaintance seemed to assume that "George" and I knew each other and I noticed that he looked slightly surprised when I said that we had never met before. It was my turn to look surprised the next morning when, walking towards the Marlborough Street magistrates' court where I was engaged in a case, I ran into George again, and after we had said a few words we went our respective ways.

I thought no more about this second encounter until a few days later when I was given a surprising reminder of it. Mr. Horwell, the Chief Constable of the CID, sent for me to have a look at some forged £5 and £10 notes. They had been given to him by an informant who had had a strange story to tell. He had apparently just come back from Paris where he had come in contact with some characters who had told him that if he was interested, they could put him in touch with someone who would let him have a quantity of these notes at half their face value. He could buy as many as he liked. It is not always easy for an informant to decide where his best interest lies, but in this there seemed to be no doubt. He said that he knew someone in London who might be interested in buying some of the notes and there and then he bought one of each to take back with him.

When he got to London he took the notes straight to Scotland Yard. Mr. Horwell, after consulting the Bank of England, had sent the informant back to Paris to try to find out more about the men with whom he had been in contact. However, when he got there the man with whom his contact was in touch (supposedly the supplier of the notes) was ill. Nevertheless he was taken to see him; and to cut a long story short, the next day the informant was eventually escorted to Berlin by another man whom he did not know and there was able to buy some £5 and £10 notes at half their face value. When the deal had been completed, he was taken to a station, put on a train, and sent back to Paris, whence he had returned to London. Unfortunately, never having been to Berlin before, he had no idea where he had been taken, nor who it was that had sold him the notes. I was consequently more than a little astonished by Mr. Horwell suddenly suggesting that as I knew both Paris and Berlin pretty well I should myself go over and try to locate the two gangs with whom his informant had been in touch. It seemed a fairly hopeless task. However, I said I would meet the informant and have a talk with him to see whether he could remember anything that might give us a clue as to where he had been. A little later Mr. Horwell sent for me again and said the meeting had been arranged. At one o'clock that day I was to be under the clock at Charing Cross station and to look out for a man with a newspaper under his arm and a red rose in his buttonhole.

I arrived at the appointed hour and there for the third time in four days I saw "George."

I should mention here that a little later, having discovered his name, I made a search of the records at Scotland Yard to see if anything was known about him. I was not altogether surprised by the result. I found that in the 1900s he had been a top-class criminal who had specialized in jewel robberies. He had operated a lot on the Continent, following wealthy ladies who traveled to the south of France and stealing their jewel cases. Other activities of his had included bank robberies and safe-breaking in manufacturing-jewelers' premises. He told me later, by which time we had become quite friendly, that he had gambled away two fortunes, but finally, after making a large coup, he had decided to invest the proceeds and settle for a quiet life. He was a bachelor and lived with his sister in a detached house in a respectable London suburb and was regarded by his neighbors as a gentleman living in retirement.

He smoked cigars, liked a glass of whisky, was always well dressed, and gave every appearance of being just what his neighbors took him to be. He had had several convictions, the last being in 1916, eighteen years earlier. He still had a wide circle of acquaintances in the criminal world, both in London and on the Continent, to whom he was known as Captain George.

Over a drink in a private room at the Charing Cross Hotel, George now repeated to me the story that he had told Mr. Horwell, adding such details as he could remember. His original contact in Paris was an old friend. When he saw him there on his second visit, this friend had taken him to see another man from whom George had hoped to be able to buy some more notes (with the intention, of course, of trying to help the Yard locate the source of supply). But they had found this other man ill with rheumatic fever and unable to help them. All that George could remember about the flat where they had seen him was that it was next to a building that looked like a Turkish bath. The sick man had said they would have to wait until he was better and could go to Berlin, where the notes were made. But George, seeing this as a good opportunity to try and find out a bit more about what was going on, said that he couldn't hang about in Paris indefinitely and suggested that he should pay someone to take him to Berlin so that he could buy some notes. He explained that he had a friend in England who might be prepared to buy a large quantity if he could see a few to satisfy himself about the quality of them. Eventually, after a lot of argument, and George's having to put down 3,000 francs as a gesture of good faith and to cover expenses, it was agreed that arrangements should be made for him to go to Berlin.

At noon the next day George returned to the flat and there he met a man called Moshe, who was to be his escort. That evening he and Moshe left for Berlin by train. When they got there they went by taxi to a building where in a flat on the second floor George met several men who he thought were possibly Poles or Russians. His appearance among them seemed to cause no surprise and he assumed that any friend of Moshe's was a friend of theirs. He was shown some £5 and £10 notes, of which he bought several, and was then taken back to the station by taxi and put on a train for Paris. He had been too scared, he said, both in Berlin and Paris, to show much curiosity about where he had been taken or to attempt to make a note of the two addresses.

I suggested that for a start he should tell me the name of his friend in Paris, hoping that I might be able to find out from the Sûreté whether anything was known about him, but it was no use. George was afraid that if it ever became known that he had revealed his friend's identity to the police, he would have his throat cut. He did not know which station he and Moshe had arrived at in Berlin and was vague about the length of the journey from the station to the flat. Never having been there before, he could not describe any of the streets through which they had passed, but seemed to remember that the one where the flat was situated had a long name. He also said that after getting out of the taxi they had gone under an archway and across a courtyard to reach the flat. Beside a window just inside the courtyard he had seen a cage with two canaries in it. On one side of the archway was a carpet shop and on the other a shop window with plumbing fixtures in it.

Only one other point emerged and that, as it happened, seemed to have no particular significance at the time. When Moshe handed his ticket to the inspector on the train, George had noticed that it was a Berlin–Paris return.

I again went to see Mr. Horwell and told him of my talk with George. I also said that it seemed a pretty hopeless task to expect me to find two flats with unknown addresses in two cities each almost as large as London. However, I said that I would try, and as I had a high opinion of the thoroughness of the German police, I felt my best chance of getting a lead on the case would be by starting in Berlin.

I left that same night by train and arrived the next morning.

At the Kurfurstendamm Hotel, where I took a room, I lay in the bath and pondered on the scanty information that was all I had. It is a habit of mine when I get stuck with a problem to think things over in the bath. Whether it is the solitude, the quiet, or the warm water, I don't know, but the answers to a lot of seemingly difficult questions seem to have come to me in the tranquilizing atmosphere of the bathroom.

As I reviewed the main points of George's story, they ranged themselves in this order in my mind:

1. He had given the sick man in Paris 3,000 francs to cover the expense of his being escorted to Berlin.

2. The next day at noon he had been introduced to Moshe.

3. On their arrival at the flat in Berlin it seemed apparent that he as well as Moshe was expected.

4. The ticket that Moshe showed the inspector was a return ticket from Berlin to Paris. (It was only now, lying in the bath, that I saw the importance of its being a return ticket.)

From these four points I drew certain conclusions: George's insistence on going to Berlin had induced the sick man in Paris to contact his Berlin associates *that same day*. How otherwise could Moshe have appeared the following morning? For it seemed highly likely from his having a Berlin–Paris *return* ticket that he must have come to Paris overnight. This left unanswered a question that seemed to have significant possibilities. How was contact made with Moshe—by telephone or telegram?

I decided to go along to the Police Headquarters on the Alexanderplatz and there I saw the Chief of the Criminal Police, Herr Otto Nebe. After I had explained my business, he took me to Meet Dr. Zauche and Herr Schulz, who were in charge of operations against currency forgers and counterfeiters throughout the whole of the German Reich. During the next few years, incidentally, up to the outbreak of war in 1939, I was to work with these two gentlemen on a good many occasions, both in Germany and England. If I may digress for a moment, it was through them that I was invited to various functions at which I met Hitler, Goering, Himmler, and other leading Nazis. At the Olympic Games in 1936 I was invited to a special stand behind Hitler's enclosure and at Himmler's invitation I visited the Gestapo headquarters in Prinz Albrechtstrasse, where I was shown round by Heydrich. It was not simply personal curiosity that prompted these visits. They enabled me to see and learn a good deal about what was going on, particularly with regard to the Nazi's anti-Jewish activities.

To return to my discussion with Nebe, Zauche, and Schulz, their views on the possibility of locating the flat to which Moshe had taken George and where he had bought his forged notes was the same as mine—that it would be like looking for a needle in a haystack. However, I had by this time formed a possible plan of action which I now put to the three of them. Whether the sick man in Paris had contacted his friends in Berlin by telegram or whether by telephone, it was, of course, impossible to say. But if he had done so by telegram this might provide us with a useful lead. In other words, if every telegram that had come from Paris on the day in question were to be examined and inspection made of the texts and the addresses to which they had been sent, we might, if we were lucky, find some that would give us a lead to the place George had described. It was obviously a very long shot, but Herr Nebe said he thought there would be no difficulty about putting the idea into operation, so off we went to the Central Post Office.

To my surprise, without any of the formalities with which such a proposal would have been greeted at the GPO in London, we were told that arrangements for inspection of the telegrams would be made at once. There was only one snag: all cables and telegrams from abroad were received on tape which was stored on reels. The length of each reel was about 1½ kilometers, or a little over a mile, and to sort out the telegrams received from Paris on the day in question would necessitate our examining twenty-two reels, or approximately twenty-odd miles of tape.

The process of examination was somewhat tedious as it meant unwinding every tape by hand, examining it inch by inch, and then rewinding it. It took the three of us from eight o'clock the next morning until six in the evening, except for a short break at midday, to pick out some twenty telegrams which looked as though they might yield results. I felt decidedly weary by this time, but I was also keen to find out whether any of the addresses we had got could be identified with George's description; so after grouping the twenty that we had picked out into various districts we started off in a taxi.

The eleventh address on the list was in a working-class district. It was 10 Nettelbeckstrasse—a street with a long name, just as George had said—and the approach to it was through an archway leading to a courtyard surrounded by flats. In the window of the porter's lodge beside the entrance was hanging a cage with two canaries in it. On either side of the entrance were the two shops described by George.

Our next move further increased my respect for the efficiency of German police methods. We went to the local police station where I found that as in all police districts in Germany, an index was kept of every house, flat, shop, office, and so on, which recorded the persons living or working there. On the card referring to No. 10 Nettelbeckstrasse the names of the occupants of the second floor flat were written in red, unlike those of the occupants of other flats. I asked why this was. The reason was as simple as it seemed to me sensible: the name of anyone with a criminal record was entered in red, the rest in black. Another index gave details about each red entry and when we turned up the cards for the second-floor occupants of No. 10, we found they were all of Russian or Polish origin and had convictions for forgery of bank notes, counterfeiting, and other crimes.

By this time it was about ten o'clock, so I invited Dr. Zauche and Herr Schulz to have dinner with me to celebrate the successful conclusion of our labors. On the walls of the restaurant where we dined were pictures of university students dueling. Herr Schulz said that in spite of a law forbidding duels, they still took place and if I would care to watch one he would take me to Berlin University to watch students fighting. I wondered what would happen in England to someone in my position if he were known to have lent encouragement to an illegal practice. In Germany it seemed they were more lenient than they would have been at home.

Again I must digress for a moment. A day or so later, curious to see what happened, I went with Herr Schulz and watched some youths fighting with swords, slashing at each other's faces. There was no question of enmity between them: they fought merely to prove their courage and their ability to endure pain without flinching. It seemed to me a pity that a less dangerous and less barbarous method could not be thought of to proclaim their manhood, but I felt that it was not for me to say so, seeing that Herr Schultz's face was scarred in several places; one scar running across his nose and cheek had needed, so he said, twenty-four stitches. He explained that in Germany a scarred face was a sign that a man had been to a university. I told him that in London it was more likely to indicate a gangster whom a rival had slashed with a razor or a broken bottle. I don't think the comparison was much appreciated.

However, to return to the investigation: the day after we had located the flat in Nettelbeckstrasse it was raided by the police. A quantity of forged £10 notes was found, together with plates and paper for printing them. Six men were arrested, among them the engravers of the plates. The other four were only traffickers. Of the two engravers, both of whom were Russians, one was called Miassojedoff, an artist by profession, who was well known to the police in various Continental countries. I was interested to meet him because I knew that he was regarded as one of the cleverest bank-note forgers in Europe.

The other man, called Smolianoff, who was also an artist, had for some time been associated with Miassojedoff and had had a number of convictions in various countries for uttering counterfeit bank notes.

Before I left Berlin there was one loose end that I wanted to tie up. The telegram from Paris in which Moshe was asked to go there (and by which only 1,000 of George's 3,000 francs had been forwarded) was signed with the name Agapev, presumably that of the man with rheumatic fever. I suggested that we should have a further search at the Central Post Office to see if any reply had been sent from Berlin. If so, it would probably tell us Agapev's address. So another search was made and once again we were lucky; a form was found which was addressed to Agapev, and armed with this I left for Paris.

As soon as I got there I went to the Sûreté and saw the
director, Monsieur Mondanel. After I had told him the whole
story he sent some officers to Agapev's address, but he and the
other occupants of the flat had disappeared. It seemed pretty
clear that somehow they had got wind of the arrest of their
friends in Berlin and were taking no chances. (Incidentally,
George had been slightly adrift in saying the flat was next to a
Turkish bath, though the mistake was perhaps understandable.
It was next to a mosque.) In the end the law caught up with
Agapev. In April 1940 I was in Paris on another investigation
when he and some others were arrested for forging passports
and identity papers, for which at that time there was a considerable demand by stateless persons who had got into France
illegally, usually to seek asylum, after the outbreak of war.

In February 1936, two years after they had been arrested,
Miassojedoff and Smolianoff were tried with their accomplices
for forging and uttering £5 and £10 notes, and in March I
went to Berlin to give evidence. Being used to the procedure in
English criminal courts and to the English rules of evidence,
I found the German procedure markedly different. There were
three professional judges, with whom two layman also sat, but
there was no jury—the verdict was decided by these five. At
certain criminal trials, including those concerning forgery and
coining, the public were not admitted. When I was called to
give evidence I found rather to my surprise that I did not have
to take the oath. Apparently it was assumed that like George
Washington, a police officer could not tell a lie. I started to
give my evidence according to the English rules of procedure,
but was stopped and told that I was to tell the court simply
what I heard from my informant. (In England, of course, hear-
say evidence is entirely forbidden.) During my evidence, defending counsel frequently interrupted with questions that led
to arguments in which everybody joined and from time to
time the atmosphere became quite heated. During one of these
outbursts I sat down for nearly half an hour while discussion
raged. The climax was reached when one of the accused who
had challenged something I was saying was rebuked by the
President of the court, who asked how he, a man with a crim-

inal record, dared to dispute the evidence of a police officer. I had seen this kind of thing in French courts, but had imagined that the more stolid German temperament would make the atmosphere of the German courtroom more like that of an English criminal court. I hope I am not a chauvinist. I have lived a good deal abroad and have close ties with a number of foreign countries, but I feel bound to say that in respect of judicial procedure both the German and the French courts seem to have much to learn from our own system, with its absence of hysteria and its safeguards against the creation of undue prejudice against the accused.

At noon on March 7, the court adjourned and I went to a restaurant nearby to have lunch. To my surprise, when I came in everybody was sitting still and silent and the waiters were standing motionless. At that moment loudspeakers round the room announced that the Führer was about to speak. The gist of his tirade, as it very soon became, was that at that very moment German troops were marching into the Rhineland. When he had finished, "Deutschland Über Alles" and the "Horst Wessel" were played and everybody stood "heiling" Hitler with the utmost enthusiasm. I never felt so lonely.

When I went back to the court I was told that the judges wanted to see me. Then the counsel and others wanted to do so, all in order to ask what I thought the British would do. It seemed to be generally accepted that the French would react strongly. I said that at the moment I could give no opinion. I might have added that I was much too preoccupied about what I should do if military action was taken by the French and British.

I finished giving evidence that afternoon, but decided that in spite of the crisis I would stay on and hear the verdicts. In the event, all the accused were found guilty and Miassojedoff and Smolianoff were each sentenced to five years' penal servitude.

Two years later I had occasion to go to Berlin again to investigate another case of forgery and arrangements were made for me to visit both men, as I wanted to ask them some questions. They were in Brandenburg Prison, some thirty miles

outside Berlin, which was in those days a modern penal establishment. Apart from its interior security—heavy steel gates in
the corridors had to be unlocked and locked again for anybody
to get in or out—it had an inner and outer perimeter wall on
which guards were posted with machine guns. Between these
walls there was a high wire fence which at night was electrified
along the top, and Alsatian dogs roamed the area between the
two walls, which was floodlit during the hours of darkness. No
prison visitors were allowed, nor was there any remission of
sentence for good conduct. The governor remarked to me
somewhat grimly that prison was a place for punishment and
prisoners had to behave themselves. I do not know the comparative statistics of crime in Germany and Britain at that time,
but I should be surprised if the deterrent effects of imprisonment were not more marked in Germany than they were here.
And I am quite sure of one thing: if precautions against escape
similar to those I saw at Brandenburg more than thirty years
ago had been adopted here, the rate of escape from British
prisons would be far lower than it has been and the enormous
effort and expense involved in belated efforts to patch up our
outworn security systems would have been saved, to the
advantage of the taxpayer and society in general.

On this visit to Berlin I found Miassojedoff and Smolianoff
painting religious pictures on the ceiling of the prison chapel.
It seemed an ironical turn of events for the two most skilled and
troublesome forgers in Europe. In the course of a long talk
with Miassojedoff he told me that before the Russian revolution, as well as being an artist he had been an officer in the
Imperial Army and later was in Denikin's White Army fighting
the Bolsheviks in the Crimea. Smolianoff had been one of his
pupils and when British and American aid was withdrawn
from Russia they had begun to engrave and print British and
American currency notes. After the defeat of Denikin's Army
they escaped together across the Black Sea to Constantinople
and then made their way through the Balkans to Germany.
They had kept some of their forged plates and from time to
time had printed some money. That someone had been doing
so, we were well aware and the purpose of my inquiries was to

find out if any of these plates still existed. But to this question my Russian friends returned only polite smiles. When we parted I did not think it likely that I should ever see or hear of them again—Miassojedoff was more than sixty years old and Smolianoff over forty—but as I have said already, crime and coincidence often seem to go hand in hand.

Less than two years later we were at war with Germany and all the evil resources of the Nazi intellect were put to devising every means of disrupting Britain's resistance. In 1940, Reinhard Heydrich, then Himmler's deputy as head of the Gestapo, began to look into the possibility of counterfeiting Bank of England notes (that is, notes to the value of £5 or more). They were to be produced in vast quantities with the aim of undermining the value of the British currency by circulating them in neutral countries. These notes were to be such exact replicas that not even English experts would be able to detect them as forgeries. This meant that extreme care would have to be taken not only about the manufacturing of the paper and the printing, but also about the system of numbering. Forging bank notes is a complicated business even for the counterfeiter who produces no more than a few notes at a time. To mount a fraudulent operation on the scale of the plan that Heydrich had in mind involved enormous scientific and numerical problems. With the Germans' usual thoroughness, some English bank-note paper was submitted to prolonged scientific examination and eventually, after experiments lasting many months, a paper was produced that was good enough to pass muster once it had been imprinted with the English watermark.

The hardest part in forging English bank notes is always the engraving of Britannia's figure in the medallion, so the finest engravers in Germany were put to the task and after working for several months from a projection ten times larger than the original, they eventually produced a perfect engraving.

These problems were difficult enough, but no less difficult was the allocation of serial numbers. This, in the days before computers, was a gigantic operation and involved the preparation of some 300 series of notes, each including numbers up to 100,000.

By the middle of 1941 all these difficulties had been overcome and the first batches of notes were put in circulation. From then onwards production increased and a special printing plant was set up in a wing of the notorious Sachsenhausen concentration camp not far from Kassel. On an average, some 200,000 notes of face values of £5, £10, £20, and £50 were printed every month and used in financial transactions carried out through neutral countries.

In 1944 it was decided to start printing 50- and 100-dollar bills and Smolianoff was brought out of obscurity to work on this project. His reputation as one of the world's outstanding forgers was quickly justified. He soon produced plates for forging the bills, but the Germans, rather uncharacteristically, neglected to take enough care in manufacturing the paper and the first batch of bills, which were perfect so far as the printing was concerned, were easily detectable because of the poor quality of the paper.

In May 1945, with the approach of the American forces, the men who operated the printing plant were ordered to destroy the workshop and the machinery and any unused paper, but bills already printed, together with plates, records, and so on, were loaded onto lorries and with the inmates of the camp were driven away. After many hold-ups and breakdowns the lorries reached the lake at Toplitsee in southern Germany and all the material was dumped into its depths. A few days later the Americans caught up with the prisoners from Sachsenhausen, whose guards had fled as the troops approached. But Smolianoff was no longer among the prisoners. He had quietly disappeared before the Americans arrived.

Nothing further was heard of him and it was later rumored that he had reached Italy, then that he was in Czechoslovakia, then in Poland. At one time it was even said that he had put himself and his plates at the service of the Russians. But his story did not end there. Of Miassojedoff I had no news and presumed he had been liquidated.

After we first met in 1934, I saw George from time to time for "business" reasons and through him got to know a friend of his whom I will call James. Like George, James had traveled a lot and had a wide circle of acquaintances in various parts of Europe. Occasionally James brought me forged £1 notes that were apparently being made in France and from the information that he gave, the French and English police were eventually able to track and arrest the forgers, who were operating in Marseilles. In 1949 James brought me some forged dollar bills of various denominations which he said were being printed in Marseilles by a gang of Corsicans. I passed this information and the forged bills on to the United States authorities and later two members of the American secret service specialists in currency offenses, came to see me. I gave them such information as I had had from James meanwhile and they then went on to Paris to consult with the Sûreté. Later they went to Marseilles with the French police, where a number of Corsicans were arrested. At the same time a cache of forged bills was found, packed ready for distribution and amounting to a face value of some four million dollars.

On their way back to Washington the two American officials called on me to thank me for my assistance and to tell me about the success of their investigations. Looking at some photographs which they showed me of various men who had been arrested I saw two faces that I recognized at once: those of my old friends, Miassojedoff and Smolianoff. I asked what had happened to them. The Americans said that neither of them was of importance; they were just odd-job men who had swept the place up and done various chores. And so they were not detained. It was clear that as artists in deception their skill was not confined to forging notes. Naturally I told the Americans what I knew and I have often wondered since whether they in turn told the story to their superiors in Washington.

Three of a
Kind
(4)

It may seem paradoxical, but I think it true, that when one has to investigate a type of crime or occurrence with which one is not familiar, it is sometimes easier to find a solution than in the more humdrum sort of case, where the probabilities are many and possible motives and suspects are equally numerous. To be faced with an out-of-the-way sort of problem in an unfamiliar locality sharpens one's wits and observation. By a coincidence—and I have said before that coincidence runs like a thread through detective work—three such cases, all of them somewhat gruesome, came my way within little more than a year between October 1938 and November 1939. Equally odd was the fact that in each case the probable truth looked very different at the end of the investigation from what seemed likely at the beginning.

At the end of October 1938 I was promoted to Detective Chief Inspector and appointed to the Murder Squad. Three weeks before my appointment I was sent to Paris to investigate the forgery of some Bank of England notes circulating in France. On the way back to England I had the roughest Channel crossing I ever had to suffer. I didn't know it at the time, of course, but the gale and the mountainous seas were to have a bearing on events which I was to be concerned with a little later.

Soon after I had joined the Murder Squad, the Sunday papers reported what was referred to as "The Riddle of the Sands." The headless body of a naked woman had been found on the beach at Perranporth on the north coast of Cornwall. The circumstances pointed to her having been murdered. She was described as being young, with beautifully manicured hands, and obviously didn't belong to the working class.

The Cornish County police asked at once for Scotland Yard's assistance and an hour or so after reading the story in the papers I was on my way to Perranporth with Detective Sergeant (later Deputy Commander) Spooner.

As soon as we arrived at Truro we went to the mortuary to have a look at the body. After what we had read in the papers, what we saw came as something of a shock. A local pathologist had pickled the remains in formalin and mounted them on a tailor's dummy. The remains consisted of the trunk, arms, hands, and thighs from which most of the flesh had rotted away. The internal organs had gone, too, and the ends of the thigh bones looked as though they had been sawn through.

Crime reporters from London were already on the spot propounding various theories, among them that the woman had been murdered, that her head had been cut off to prevent identification, and the body then buried in a shallow grave in the sand, from which it had been washed out by successive tides. Crime reporters are a hard-working race. Theirs is a round-the-clock job, a continual race against time to get their copy in before their papers go to press, and a continual struggle to keep abreast with hour-to-hour developments. When this affair broke, major crime news was scarce, the weather was mild and pleasant, and Perranporth an attractive seaside place.

For the crime reporters this assignment was no doubt a pleasant break and their one objective was to keep the story alive for as long as possible in the expectation of sensational developments.

I was not concerned with their views on the case. I was there to try and find out the facts about it. And some of them, as things turned out, were distinctly surprising. It takes a lot to surprise a detective. He soon becomes conditioned, if he is any good, to startling or unusual phenomena. But I must confess I was surprised by what I learned about local habits and customs.

Perranporth beach is about four miles long. Some two weeks earlier a woman walking along the beach had seen the woman's headless body lying on the sand just about the high-tide watermark. She told me when I interviewed her that apart from the head being missing, the body was complete and seemed to be well preserved although the skin was pink. She had reported the discovery to the local policeman, who had set out to look for the body, but by that time it was dark and raining and he failed to find it. Possibly it had been dragged out to sea by the high tide and afterwards was washed back again, because the next day it was back on the sands, where it was seen at different times by several people walking along the beach. During the next ten days it was seen lying in the same spot by a number of people whom I interviewed. In their daily perambulations along the beach they apparently used to look out for it and described to me the changes they had noticed and the gradual disintegration of the body. After two or three days in the sunshine it had become swollen, then the skin broke, the body began to break up and seagulls started to peck at the flesh until gradually the legs and feet disappeared. No one that I talked to had thought it worthwhile telling the local policeman about the body. One thought it had been buried at sea. Others said it was not unusual for human remains to be washed up on the beach and regarded the matter as being of no particular interest. Indeed, one or two expressed surprise at the "fuss" about the body, and I began to realize that as a townsman I would have to make allowances for the views of those living by the sea, especially on the coast of Cornwall, with its stories of shipwrecks and wreckers going back through the centuries.

Even the recovery of what was left of the body seemed to have occurred only by chance. The woman who had first seen it happened to be visiting her doctor two weeks later and had mentioned it to him and after he had finished his surgery he had gone to the beach and there found the remains. He had first thought of burying them in the sand, then decided to telephone the local constable. He in turn went down to the beach, found the remains, and stuffed them in a sack which he had put in his garden shed for the night. Later that evening, then being off duty, he had gone to the local pub, which was also a hotel, where he had mentioned the matter. It so happened that the licensee had at one time been a Flat Street photographer. Hearing the story, he had rung up various London newspapers and given them a highly colored account of the events, and had said, with an eye to business, that he would reopen the hotel, which had been shut down for the winter, to accommodate any reporters who might come down. This undoubtedly was the cause of the sensational news in the Sunday papers and the arrival of a crowd of crime reporters before we reached the scene.

The man most surprised by all this was the Cornish Chief Constable. The first he knew of the affair was what he had read in the Sunday papers, and after hearing some details from his superintendent at Truro, he decided to call in Scotland Yard.

Several lines of investigation presented themselves. First, I had inquiries made to see whether any women were missing from any of the houses, hotels, or boarding houses in the county, but these inquiries turned out to be negative. Next, searches were made along the sand dunes to see if any women's clothing had been hidden there. The result, if surprising, was not very helpful; various pairs of knickers were found, some of them stuffed down rabbit holes and hidden in other places.

It occurred to me that parts of the body might have been carried off by seagulls and in searching for anything they might have got hold of, as well as in looking for clothing, I found plenty of helpers among the local people. This resulted in most of the leg and foot bones being recovered, but not the skull. From what I had learned so far it seemed unlikely that the body had been cut up, but having great faith in Sir Bernard Spilsbury, the Home Office pathologist, I asked him to come down and have a look at the remains. In view of how little he had to work on—a rib cage with the right arm and hand attached to it, though with the flesh much decayed, and the thigh and leg bones—his conclusions, judging from later events, were astonishingly accurate. The marks on the ends of the thigh bones, which seemed to suggest they had been sawn through, were due, he said, to friction with the sand when the body had been drawn back and forth by the changing tides. After he had made his examination, he went back to London and soon afterwards we had his report.

His conclusions were that the woman must have been in her middle thirties, was about 5 feet 2 inches in height, had never done any manual work, nor worn a ring on her right hand. He also gave her approximate weight.

The flesh of the right hand was still intact, although exposure had caused it to become loose, swollen, and wrinkled and some adipocere had set in (that is, a fatty substance that appears in dead bodies subjected to moisture). This had caused the ridges that form fingerprints to disappear. However, I thought I would ask Chief Superintendent Cherrill (then in charge of the Fingerprint Section at Scotland Yard) to see if there was any possibility of getting at least one fingerprint from the hand, so that he could search his records to see if the woman were known to the police. Cherrill came down to Truro, but when he saw the hand he said it would be impossible to take prints in the usual way, so he decided to try and peel the skin off the fingers. As the skin was rotten this was an extremely delicate and painstaking operation which I believe had never been tried before, but Cherrill did it successfully. He took the skin back to London, treated it, and the next day telephoned to say that he had been able to take good prints. But all this came to nothing. The records were searched but no trace of the woman was found.

In the meantime Spooner and I had been busy in other directions. There were some disused tin mines in the area which drained into the sea, and we had packages dropped down them to see if they could be washed out onto the beach. While this was being done I happened to see two boys walking along the sands, obviously looking for something. I asked them if they were taking part in the searches I had organized, but they said they were looking for drift bottles. These, it seemed, were bottles set adrift as part of an experiment organized by the Ministry of Agriculture and Fisheries in connection with the movements of tides and currents. Anyone finding one of the bottles, if he filled in a card that was inside, saying where and when the bottle was found, was entitled to a reward of 2s.

Since the beginning of my inquiries almost everyone I had interviewed in their homes had invited me to have a glass of wine. During my seven years in Brussels I had acquired a taste for wine and what I was now offered was obviously a very good burgundy, although the bottles were of all kinds and shapes. In view of what I had discovered about flotsam and jetsam in that part of Cornwall, I felt it might be indiscreet to ask where so much good wine came from, but I formed my own conclusions.

My conversation with the two boys on the beach, together with this plentiful supply of wine, opened up a new line of thought. I found on making inquiries that a number of barrels had been washed up on the beach a few days before I arrived. It seemed that these had aroused a good deal more interest than the dead body. From further inquiries I found that out of 145 drift bottles dumped in mid-Channel, seventy-nine had come ashore at Perranporth. I also learned that on that stormy day of my journey from Paris, a French boat with a cargo of wine had been wrecked on one of the Channel Islands and pounded to pieces. This was at about the same time as the drift bottles had been dropped into the Channel. So it was clear that during a period of some four weeks a number of barrels from the wreck and also a number of drift bottles had traveled along the Channel to Land's End and round the

Cornish coast up to Perranporth, carried there by winds, tides, and currents.

With this in mind I next got hold of some sea charts and after discussing currents, tides, winds, weather conditions, sea temperatures, and so on with various experts, I asked for inquiries to be made to see if we could find out whether a woman was missing from anywhere along the coast between Dover and Land's End, and also from any boats or ships in the Channel. As a result, I discovered that six weeks earlier a woman had been reported missing from a liner in mid-Channel on a voyage from Canada to England. She was a single woman who had been living with relatives in the Midlands, and had gone to Canada some months before. However, she had been refused permission to land because she seemed to be of unsound mind and had been sent back to England in the same liner. There was no doubt that she had disappeared overboard, possibly as the result of an accident, though in view of her mental state suicide seemed more likely.

The woman's relatives provided details of her appearance that corresponded with remarkable similarity to Sir Bernard Spilsbury's estimate of the age, height, and weight of the woman whose body had been found on the beach. They said furthermore that she had never done any manual work, nor worn a ring. When told that the remains that had been found might be those of their missing relation, they refused to accept this theory, one of them making the rather surprising remark that identification of the remains would involve the expense of a funeral. We did ask, however, if they would allow Cherrill to examine the bedroom which the missing woman had occupied before she went to Canada and to this they agreed. Cherrill then examined the whole room in an endeavor to find some fingerprints for comparison with those of the corpse, but he told me afterwards that he had never examined a room that had been cleaned so scrupulously. Every piece of wood had been thoroughly polished, and floors, walls, doors, china, and glass so carefully dusted or washed that not a single fingerprint of any sort could he find anywhere.

The whole of this inquiry lasted ten days, during which long and detailed discussions took place with the Home Office, the Board of Trade, the Admiralty, the Air Ministry, and the Ministry of Agriculture and Fisheries, as well as with the local authorities. The *Daily Telegraph* in reporting the case, in which an open verdict was recorded, said, "It is doubtful whether any death mystery investigated by the police has necessitated so much technical information and quasi-scientific inquiry"—a view of the case with which I would wholeheartedly agree.

Almost a year after this Perranporth case, in 1939, just after the War had started, I was awakened in the middle of the night by the telephone. The Chief Constable of Leicestershire had asked for the Yard's help in investigating what was believed to be the discovery of the dismembered bodies of two women and four babies which had been found near a bungalow outside Leicester.

Taking a detective sergeant with me, I caught an early train and was met at Leicester by the local detective superintendent, who took us up to the place where the bodies had been found some miles outside the town.

A few yards from the bungalow a pit had been dug and beside it in a tin bath and loose on the ground was a collection of human legs, arms, a heart or two, kidneys, livers, and other organs, and also what appeared to be the bodies of four babies. As I examined them I noticed the same pungent smell that I had noticed in the mortuary at Truro—the smell of formalin.

I was told that two boys had been prowling round the bungalow at about ten o'clock the night before—a pitch-black night, raining and windy—when one of them had tripped over something. The other had struck a match to see what it was, and found that it was a human leg. He had dropped it at once and run to the police station. A policeman had gone to the spot and after flashing his torch around had reported to his senior officers what he thought he had seen—the dismembered bodies of two women and four babies by an open grave.

I came to the conclusion at once that these various odds and ends were medical specimens or exhibits and that the "babies" were fetuses, probably from miscarriages. However, the local police doctor did not agree. He thought the remains were those of two full-term babies that had had a separate existence and had died some time after birth. So once again I asked Sir Bernard Spilsbury to come and give us his opinion.

Before he arrived—it was on a Sunday morning—I had almost finished my inquiries. The bungalow belonged to a local doctor, who was apparently most assiduous in his work and studies. When I interviewed him his story was a simple one. When he had a patient who, for one reason or another, had had to have a limb amputated, he had kept the limb and pickled it with the intention of dissecting it later. Whenever he helped at an autopsy he did the same thing with some of the organs from the body. And he did the same when one of his women patients had a miscarriage. All these specimens he kept in a cupboard in his house, but when war broke out, his wife had wanted the cupboard to store food, anticipating that it would be rationed. So the doctor cleared out the cupboard and took its contents to his bungalow outside the town, where he dug a pit to bury everything; but with the bad weather and night coming on, he was unable to finish the operation and had left everything there, intending to return on Sunday morning to finish the job. In fact, he still had some more fetuses in his garage. So far as I was concerned the only thing left to clear up was the question raised by the police doctor.

I met Sir Bernard Spilsbury on his arrival and explained the circumstances to him, and then we went to an infirmary outside the town where the remains had been sent to the mortuary.

As I have said, I had a great respect for Sir Bernard, as did every police officer who came in contact with him. He was always courteous, kind, and considerate and ready to listen and discuss cases in which we were concerned. At an autopsy he would always explain clearly the importance of what he brought to light during his examination. Having been present at a good many of his autopsies and having watched him and listened to his comments, I had gained some considerable knowledge of human anatomy and pathology. After we had spent two hours discussing the remains, Sir Bernard confirmed my view that none of the fetuses had had a separate existence. And so the assiduous doctor was vindicated, though I felt bound to agree with Sir Bernard's opinion that he was "a curious man."

Almost as soon as I got back from Leicester, I was on my travels again, this time to Margate, where part of a woman's body had been found in the corporation dust destructor. The police surgeon's opinion was that the spine had been sawn through, and also the legs above the knees. The case was therefore being treated as one of murder and Scotland Yard had been asked to assist in the investigation.

As at Leicester, the Chief Constable met us and took us to the local mortuary to see the remains. They consisted of a complete pelvis attached to the five lumbar and last dorsal vertebrae and the two femurs, or thigh bones. The pelvis was covered with a mass of decomposed flesh extending down to the femurs below the hip bones. The spinal column looked as though it had been cut through and there was what also looked like a deep cut between the dorsal and first lumbar vertebrae. The thigh bones were quite white and had been separated cleanly at the knee joints. They had the appearance, as had one of the hip bones, of having been roughly sandpapered.

These marks seemed something like those on the bones I had seen at Perranporth, the result of the body having been washed up and down on the beach. So I asked what the beach at Margate was like and was told that it was also sandy and washed by tidal waters.

After we left the mortuary we went to the dust destructor where its mechanics were explained to us. The refuse when it arrived was shot into a hopper. Metallic refuse was sorted mechanically, rags, bottles, and bones by a team of men working on either side of a rotary belt, and anything left over passed into furnaces for destruction. The conveyor belt had been started at 3 A.M. the previous morning and the first lot of garbage to be dealt with had been collected the day before from the Westgate area. Watching the refuse go through the feed gate, the man in charge had seen a mass of flesh with two large bones sticking out of it.

A sorter on the conveyor belt had seized it as it came out on to the belt and as it was rather large and the bones of a type he had not seen before, he put it aside and called his foreman, who, having been through a first-aid course, recognized the remains as being human. He took them to the Medical Officer of Health, who sent them to the mortuary and then informed the police.

I next made inquiries about the collection of refuse on the sea front and the beach and found that it was collected every day and dumped into bins which were emptied periodically by the dustmen. I then saw the man who had cleared the bins two days before. He remembered a mass of flesh with two bones sticking out of it which he had emptied from a bin on the promenade, but whether they were human or animal bones he just didn't know, but he had slung them into his cart, which was emptied into the dust destructor later that afternoon.

The next person I interviewed was the beach scavenger, who told me that four days before, on November 6, a policeman had asked him to get rid of some bones on the beach in West Bay. He found them there and adhering to them a mass of decomposed flesh which had a woolly covering. Thinking it was part of a dead sheep, he put it in the bin on the promenade for collection by the refuse cart.

The mention of this woolen covering puzzled me. There was no wool on the remains I had seen at the mortuary, though it might well have been stripped off while they were going through the destructor.

Next I interviewed the policeman who had spoken to the scavenger, and then another policeman whom he had relieved. Both of them had seen the remains lying on the beach at different times. The second constable said that on the afternoon of October 20 a boy had reported to him that there was part of a human body on the beach. He had examined what he found and, like the scavenger, thought from the woolen fleece attached to it that it was part of a sheep. Round the flesh was a strip of whitish gray material about three inches wide, which was kept in place by a knotted cord. He cut the cord and removed the strip of material, which came to pieces in his hand. The lower edge of the strip was quite straight, but the upper edge was irregular, as if it had been torn off. He could not suggest what the cord or the material, which he had thrown away, could be. After consulting his sergeant, who also thought the remains were those of a sheep, he threw them back into the sea.

Since then the remains had been seen by several people at various places along the beach, but not until November 6 did anyone report the matter to the police. That morning a young man told a policeman that there was part of a human body on the beach in West Bay, but when he went to look at it, the policeman recognized it as his "old acquaintance, the sheep."

The next day he went to the mortuary and saw the remains. Although there was no "wool" on them, he identified them as those he had seen on October 20 and November 6.

After interviewing the two constables, I saw the boy who first found the remains. He was aged thirteen and lived in London, but his school had been evacuated to Margate. He described very clearly and precisely the condition of the remains and how, after reporting the matter to the police, he had watched the constable examining them.

At the end of our first day's inquiries I went to see the Chief Constable. I told him all that I had been able to discover and explained the similarities between the bone scarifications and those I had noticed at Perranporth. I said that if the police doctor were agreeable I would like Sir Bernard Spilsbury to examine the remains with a view to his giving some indication of the dead woman's age and any other details he might be able to discover. I still could not find any explanation of the gray woolen substance, which had been described as thick and fluffy, and therefore unlikely to be a piece of clothing.

Our discussion was interrupted at this point by the news that lifeboats were bringing in survivors from a ship that had been sunk by a magnetic mine in the Thames Estuary. An emergency plan already established was immediately put into operation and I went with the Chief Constable to the port to meet the boats landing the survivors.

Watching the poor chaps as they were brought ashore, I noticed that they were all wearing lifebelts of thickly padded canvas webbing which covered their chests and backs and were fastened by a strong cord round the body. Although I had traveled in many ships, it had never occurred to me to look at a lifebelt and I asked what they were filled with. I was told it was kapok—a fine cotton wool.

I had already arranged for searches and inquiries to be made along the beaches on both sides of the Thames Estuary from Ennis Bay to the North Foreland Lighthouse to find out whether any other parts of a body had been seen or washed up, but without result. I now asked that if a lifebelt should be found it should be brought to me. The very next morning I was presented with one that had been found in St. Mildred's Bay. The shoulder straps were damaged and sodden kapok was protruding through a tear in the canvas webbing. I ripped open the webbing still further and the kapok swelled out, looking just like a sheep's fleece. The schoolboy and both constables, when I showed them the kapok, said without any hesitation that it was similar to what they had seen on the remains. The constable who had thrown them back into the sea had no doubt that the strip of material underneath the cord was similar to the bottom edge of the front of the lifebelt.

When I saw the police doctor I told him what I had established, and that the apparent saw marks on the bones were probably caused by the friction of the sand, but he was not convinced. He was also reluctant to suggest how long the woman had been dead. However, when I suggested tactfully that I would like to have Sir Bernard Spilsbury's opinion, he was perfectly agreeable. Sir Bernard came down from London the next day and made his examination. He concluded that the remains were those of a woman of about 4 feet 11 inches tall, of poor muscular development, and probably between twenty-five and forty years old. The lower ends of the thigh bones had been worn down on each side by friction against some rough surfaces, possibly shingle or rocks. There was nothing to indicate the cause of death, but the amount of adipocere pointed to the body having been in the water for about two or three months. There was nothing to suggest that the remains had been prepared or used as an anatomical specimen and no signs that a saw or cutting instrument had been used on the bones, so it seemed probable that the body had been dismembered while it was in the sea.

We now began to inquire about tides, winds, drifts, and currents, not only from the authorities, but, as at Perranporth, from the local fishermen. We were told that if a body were in the Thames it would be carried down and probably come ashore on the southern bank about twenty miles west of Margate. But if it were to pass beyond that point, the chances were that it would be carried by currents towards the northern bank of the Thames Estuary, and unless it were washed ashore in the neighborhood of Shoeburyness would be carried northwards towards the Blackwater. Anything entering the Black Deep Channel east of Foulness would be carried by currents and tides into the North Sea.

I discovered through inquiring about the tides that there is a main tidal water south of the line Orford Ness—North Hinder Lightship which has a flow southwards of 5½ hours and an ebb of 6½ hours. This tide meets a second tide off the Goodwin Sands which has a westward flow of five hours from the Dyck Lightship off Dunkirk and an ebb of seven hours. This means that a body from the north of the Thames Estuary would be carried out to the North Sea, while a body entering the water off Margate, if not washed up fairly soon by the North Foreland or Ramsgate, would drift out towards the French or Belgian coast.

I now began making inquiries to find out what would happen to a body wearing a life jacket if it had entered the water somewhere in the North Sea, and was told that in normal circumstances it would be unlikely to appear on the north Kentish coast. However, on the day on which the remains were first seen, October 20, high water was at 5:16 A.M. and for some days before this, strong northeast winds had been blowing, which would have counteracted the ebb of tides on floating objects.

Several fishermen whom I talked to told me that bodies sometimes floated to and fro with the tides off the east coast for four or five weeks before being blown by strong northeast winds on to the north Kentish shore, where heavy seas accompanying such winds would dash the body onto the rocks. Usually being by then in an advanced state of decomposition, it would soon be broken to pieces.

At the inquest on the remains the coroner said it was impossible to establish who the woman was or when, where, or how she had died, though there could be very little doubt she was the victim of a tragedy at sea. He therefore returned an open verdict.

A week later, inquiries made along the east coast revealed that a London woman, aged thirty and about five feet in height, who had been on a holiday at Lowestoft in the middle of August, had hired a small sailing boat and that while she was out at sea a storm had blown up. Two days later the boat was found drifting, but her body had never been recovered—nor had a kapok lifebelt which was part of the boat's equipment.

A Pious
Fraud
(5)

From time to time one reads of financial crooks being prosecuted for frauds involving enormous sums of money. In these cases many people who had perhaps invested all their savings are usually ruined and left to drag out the later years of their lives in poverty. It is impossible to assess the suffering and misery resulting from this type of fraud, but when it does occur, which is fortunately not often, its results are pitiable and widespread.

Between the two world wars there flourished another type of financial fraud in which those who parted with their money did so in answer to bogus appeals to their charitable instincts. In the social conditions of the thirties, with vast numbers of unemployed and many thousands of families barely able to exist, conditions in working-class areas throughout Britain were appalling. The innumerable appeals made in the name of charity presented a harrowing picture of the circumstances in which these unfortunate families were forced to dwell. Meanwhile, the creatures who organized fraudulent appeals on their behalf made a comfortable living. Although the individual contributions were usually small, the total often amounted to hundreds of pounds a year. Most of the money that was collected went straight into the pockets of these rogues; very little, if any, went to the supposed objects of the appeals.

In 1938 I became head of a section at New Scotland Yard where, among other things, these fraudulent charities, which had developed into a serious racket, were dealt with. In my squad I had a Detective Inspector William Bray, an energetic and very thorough investigator, whose persistence and patience was unlimited, and we decided to make an intensive drive to end this type of fraud. In this not only was Bray outstandingly successful, but exposure of the extent of this racket resulted in new legislation which tightened up police powers over bogus charities. In the course of this drive Inspector Bray uncovered one of the meanest and most hypocritical rogues ever to engage in this sort of deception, operating under the cloak of the church and using the distress and poverty of those in his parish as ground for his appeals.

In 1925 Harry Clapham was appointed Vicar of St. Thomas' Church in Lambeth, London. He was born in a midlands town in 1888, went to an elementary school, and at the age of fourteen started work in a local mill. He joined the Church Army movement and was trained as one of its evangelists, but resigned shortly after the outbreak of the War in 1914 and went to Canada. There he served in churches until 1922, when he returned to England and became a curate in the north of England and later in the West Country.

His stipend as Vicar of St. Thomas' was £400 a year and his vicarage was rent free. Before coming to Lambeth his income had just been sufficient to meet his financial obligations—he was married and had two children—and when he left his parish the congregation subscribed over £100 as a parting present and a friend lent him £75 to furnish his new vicarage.

In 1926, while he was visiting a patient in St. Thomas' Hospital in Lambeth, he happened to see some girls in the almoner's office dealing with checks and postal orders sent to the hospital in answer to an appeal. Professing an interest in such matters, he asked how the appeal was organized and was told that the names and addresses of people to whom appeals were sent could be got from a certain agency at a cost of 30s a thousand. That same night Clapham wrote to the agency and asked for a list of 3,000 names and addresses. This was the beginning of what purported to be a scheme for helping poor people in the widespread and densely populated areas of his parish. In his appeals he was able to describe quite truthfully their appalling poverty.

How many individual appeals he sent out between 1926 and 1939 there was no way of discovering, but one thing is certain: they amounted to hundreds of thousands. He appealed for money, clothes, and books, and at Christmas time for toys and dolls for children. After the War broke out in 1939 he claimed in his appeals that parcels of cigarettes and chocolate were needed for servicemen and aid and gifts for impoverished mothers and children who had been evacuated to the country.

In 1941 St. Thomas' Church and parish hall were destroyed in an air raid and near by a hostel for homeless men received a direct hit which killed many people. Shortly afterwards Clapham sent out this appeal:

from REV. H. CLAPHAM, B.D., F.R.G.S.
St. Thomas' Vicarage,
82 Westminster Bridge Road,
S.E.1.

June 6th 1941
Dear ————,

I regret to report that our Parish Church and Hall, including our "Night Shelter" for homeless men, and our "Food Kitchen" for poor people, has recently been *destroyed by enemy action.* I cannot report the number of deaths, and the amount of destruction in my Parish, but many are left *homeless and in need of our help.* We are doing our best to continue the Social and Spiritual work among this mass of *10,000 poor people,* but have only two small rooms, and the "crypt" of the Church left for this purpose.

The Government and the Insurance Company will *probably* allow the amount of insurance (£15,000) towards the cost of rebuilding, but another £10,000 will be needed. Will you do what you can to help us in our *effort to rebuild after the War is over?*

In the meantime, I earnestly appeal for help to equip a "Night Shelter" for homeless old and infirm men in the "crypt" of the Church, and then give them shelter and a little food, and also equip a "Soup Kitchen" in a small room, and then provide *soup for poor and homeless people.* We need 20 mattresses and blankets for the "Shelter"; a boiler and tea urn, and tins of soup for the "Kitchen"; used shoes, clothing, and furniture for the *homeless people,* and the poor children evacuated to the country. PLEASE SEND A PARCEL TO THE ABOVE ADDRESS.

Hoping that you can and will help our efforts.

Yours sincerely,

(sgd.) H. CLAPHAM

(*Vicar of St. Thomas'*)

P.S. Last time you kindly sent:—£1.

It may be that when Clapham sent out his first appeals in 1926 he was sincere. The need to alleviate the poverty in his parish was overwhelming and the response from people all over the country was generous. Contributions ranged from a shilling or two up to £50, and over the years money poured in in increasing amounts. In fact, so much began to come in and so many things were received that the post office, the railways, and road transport firms had to make special arrangements for delivering the flood of letters and parcels.

In the middle thirties Clapham's mode of life began to change. In 1936 he visited Palestine and in 1937 Germany and Austria, traveling in a large car; in 1938 he made a trip to the United States and Canada which lasted for more than three months, and in 1939 went with his daughter for a six weeks' cruise to the West Indies. In the circles in which he now moved, good living was appreciated and just before Christmas 1938, Clapham gave a lavish party for some thirty or forty people who were entertained by three theatrical stars.

This style of living, ostensibly maintained on a stipend of £400 a year, began to cause some concern not only to the church authorities but to two people working with Clapham at St. Thomas'. One was the man who had organized the collection raised for him in his previous parish, and who, incidentally, had lent him the £75 that was to have been spent on furnishing his vicarage. Neither of these gentlemen, in spite of persistent inquiries, could get a proper explanation from Clapham as to how the money that was received was being spent, and eventually both of them left his church, feeling strongly suspicious that all was not well.

The church authorities now pressed Clapham to submit his affairs to audit and eventually he presented them with a certified balance sheet; but the authorities were still left with an uneasy feeling that things were not as they should be. In 1939 they again asked for an audit, but this time Clapham refused their request.

During that year it happened that there was a good deal of publicity about prosecutions of bogus charitable organizations and no doubt because of this we began to get letters at Scotland Yard questioning Clapham's *bona fides*.

After making some discreet inquiries and learning, too, that the church authorities were perturbed, I asked Inspector Bray to investigate the matter. As head of the section to which I had been appointed the year before, my responsibilities left no time for me to undertake long and involved day-to-day inquiries such as it seemed the investigation of Clapham's affairs would probably need. In any case, I had absolute confidence in Bray and we kept constantly in touch.

This was in December 1939. It was not until May 1942 that Clapham's financial manipulations, which had put tens of thousands of pounds into his pocket, were unraveled and he himself brought to justice.

For several days before Christmas Bray kept observation on

Clapham's vicarage and saw parcels, boxes, teachests and various other things arrive, as well as bags of mail. A large number of callers also left parcels and among these callers was a barrister whom Bray knew. Bray spoke to him and was told that for some years, in response to Clapham's appeals, which his wife had received regularly, she had sent parcels of clothing for distribution among the poor of St. Thomas' parish.

At about the same time Bray found that a sale of goods was shortly to be held at a hall next to the church. He decided to go along, taking with him another officer, both of them being in plain clothes. When they got there, about fifty women, many of them with large sacks, were sitting in the first two rows of chairs. On the stage three women were arranging the goods that were to be sold—dolls, toys, and clothing of all sorts. Presently a woman came in and the sale began. This woman, acting as an auctioneer, knocked each item down to the highest bidder. Most of the clothing—much of it looked almost new— was bought by the women in the first two rows, to the disgust of other women sitting behind, one of whom Bray heard saying that they had no chance to buy anything because of the "dealers." Occasionally the auctioneer put on a garment to show it off, in one case a coat, which although it was bid for she didn't sell, and after the sale was over, she left wearing it. Her language and behavior, especially when she had some underwear to offer, were decidedly coarse. In all, about £40 was raised during the afternoon.

Having discussed the situation with Bray, I decided that inquiries should be made into Clapham's financial position. As a result, it was found that when he took over the living the church was in debt to the tune of several hundred pounds, but that this debt had since been cleared and the interior of the church renovated at considerable expense. For example, there had been a new stained-glass window costing £450.

During the next few months it was found that in the early thirties Clapham had bought seven houses in southwest London at a total cost of over £6,000; that he had nearly £5,000 invested in building societies, and over £1,000 in Savings Certificates, and had paid nearly £2,000 in insurance premiums. In 1939 he had bought two more houses in southwest London, one for some £900 and another for £700.

During the first half of 1940 the church authorities pressed Clapham again for a thorough audit of his books, but the result was no more satisfactory than before, so I decided to call on him with Bray. Our reception, after saying who we were, was decidedly frosty. We were met first by one woman, then by another, both of whom, after a whispered consultation, said that Clapham was out. Where he had gone and when he would return they were unable to tell us. When we got back to Scotland Yard, which was only five minutes away from Lambeth, we found that Clapham had telephoned to say he was going away immediately for a short holiday.

On August 17 we made an appointment to see him, but again we were told when we got to the vicarage that he was not in. However, after some difficulty, having produced our warrant cards, we were shown into Clapham's study, where he eventually joined us.

Our call was ostensibly about a woman who had applied for a permit to make collections on his behalf. He said he did not know her and we then tried to steer the conversation round to his own charitable work, but we got nowhere. Every donation, he said, was carefully recorded and his books and accounts were audited by a qualified accountant and submitted to his bishop, who knew of what he was doing and was perfectly satisfied with his work.

However, our visit was not entirely unsatisfactory. We had at last met Clapham and sized him up. It was clear that he was by no means an ordinary clergyman. He had a staff which, judging from what we saw when he spoke to them, he controlled like an overlord, and his precautions against unexpected visitors were impressive.

Whether or not he had become aware of our inquiries I don't know. It was not unlikely, seeing that many people had been interviewed and that the church authorities were obviously dissatisfied with what he had told them about his charitable work. Be that as it may, soon after our visit he wrote to

his bishop asking for permission to apply for a chaplaincy in
the RAF or some other branch of the fighting services. This
application was refused.

At this stage the church authorities were advised to consult
an accountant, Mr. J. A. Cook, with many years of experience
in examining fraudulent accounts. After spending some two
months in going through Clapham's books he reported that
he was not satisfied with the state of affairs because the documents that had been produced were incomplete. There were,
for instance, no accounts relevant to Clapham's appeals before
1934, which was when he said he had first started them, nor
would he give Mr. Cook permission to investigate his bank
account. Nevertheless, some interesting facts were brought to
light. Between 1933 and 1938 Clapham had bought 14½ million
envelopes, half of which were prepaid. Assuming that three
envelopes a year were used for each subscriber, this indicated
that almost a million appeals were sent out per annum. One
appeal was for a "hostel for fallen women" which was found
not to exist.

The accounts for "Jumble Sales" recorded the amount taken
on December 22, 1939, as £8 7s 6d. This was the sale attended
by Bray at which some £40 had been taken. Mr. Cook estimated that roughly £1,000 a year was being taken at these
sales. In spite of his thoroughness, lacking certain documents
and having no access to Clapham's bank accounts, Mr. Cook
was unable to discover the sources from which Clapham obtained his funds, but he had no doubt that his accounts had
been falsified and that Clapham had lied to him over and over
again.

The results of all these investigations were submitted to the
Director of Public Prosecutions, but it was eventually decided
that neither the church authorities nor the police had enough
evidence to support proceedings against Clapham.

After so much hard work this was very disappointing, but
though the law was powerless, Clapham's own greed was to
bring about his downfall. Bray was not the man to give up and
he continued to keep a close watch on Clapham's activities. By
so doing he learned in due course that there existed a certain

trust which helped poor clergymen to maintain their sons at universities. Knowing that Clapham had a son at a university, Bray made inquiries of this trust and found that in February 1940, Clapham had applied for a grant to assist him in paying for his son's education. In giving certain particulars about his gross income, Clapham put down the amount of £398. In the rules that had been sent to him before he made the application, it was clearly stated that: "The income of the clergyman applying must in no case exceed £400 net from all sources . . ."

As a result of his application he was made a grant of £15 a year, payable in half-yearly sums, and in July he received a check for £7 10s 0d.

Bray had by now discovered that in addition to an income of about £700 a year from the properties he had bought, Clapham had also invested considerable sums in building societies and was believed to have deposits in several banks. Equally interesting was another discovery, namely that Clapham had applied for financial help towards the education of his son, and later for his daughter, to the trustees of another charity—The Worshipful Company of Haberdashers. A condition of assistance was that the applicant's income should not exceed £600 a year. As a result of Clapham's request, he was granted £50 a year for three years, subject to his son making satisfactory progress.

We now had evidence to prove a charge of obtaining money by false pretences and also of attempting to do so, and eventually Bray was instructed to apply at Lambeth Magistrates' Court for a summons against Clapham. However, it so happened that the magistrate to whom the application was made had been a generous contributor to Clapham's appeals and instead of granting a summons he issued a warrant for his arrest.

That same day we pulled him in. The police, searching the basement rooms of the vicarage, found them equipped like an office, with typewriters, addressing machines, index cabinets, and so on. Seven post-office mailbags containing 25,000 appeals were awaiting collection. In the index cabinets were about 25,000 names and addresses of subscribers, recording the amounts they had sent and also particulars of those who had sent clothing. Sums of money were also found, but most important of all were ledgers, books, and other documents relating to Clapham's "charitable" affairs. His house at Kingston Vale was also searched and there, too, a mass of material was found, including some postal orders and unpaid checks.

After being remanded several times, Clapham was brought to trial at the Old Bailey on April 17, 1942. The trial lasted eleven days and in spite of being strenuously defended, he was found guilty on all counts and sentenced to three years penal servitude.

During the investigations into his activities it was found that between 1925 and 1941, when his nominal income was £400 a year, he had opened ninety-one accounts with banks and building societies into which he had paid a total of £117,576. Apart from this, he had bought various properties and had also taken out a large insurance policy. Yet the temptation to get his hands on another £15 was more than he could resist. But for this, it is possible that he might have been able to evade the law indefinitely.

Making Money

(6)

☞ Coincidence, as I have indicated here and there, looms large in the imagination of a detective: something that may seem merely a coincidence to the layman automatically becomes a matter for consideration. This is well illustrated by the case in question, one of two crimes committed at different periods and in different countries, but having certain similarities that provided the missing link in a chain of evidence.

In March 1935, only five months after the end of the Miassojedoff-Smolianoff affair, Scotland Yard was warned by Dr. Zauche, of the Forgery Section of the Berlin criminal police, that forged £5 notes were being sold in the German underworld at half their face value. The forgeries were of a new and unknown type and obviously the work of an expert. I was instructed to go to Berlin to cooperate with the German police in finding out where they came from.

When I arrived in Berlin I was put in touch with the contact from whom Dr. Zauche had had his information. It was arranged that through this man I should be introduced as a possible buyer to the gang who was offering the notes for sale. I was to represent myself as an Englishman engaged in smuggling and gun-running and living in Antwerp. I knew a good deal about these sorts of matters, having been concerned with them during the time I was in Belgium as a liaison officer between Scotland Yard and the Belgian police. There would have been no point, of course, in my actually buying any of the forged notes; the idea was simply to try and find out where the plant was and who the forgers were. To do this meant that I would have to convince them that I had enough money to buy a large quantity of notes, as well as facilities for distributing them; the intention being that by keeping me under observation during negotiations, the Berlin police would be able to discover the gang's operational headquarters.

There was one ironic problem—the question of cash. The gang would obviously want to see the color of my money before engaging in serious talk, and the German police, like the English, don't have unlimited sums to play about with. It was Dr. Zauche who hit on the solution. He produced a quantity of forged 50 and 20 reichsmark notes which I made up into packets with layers of genuine notes on the top and bottom.

My contact duly introduced me to the gang, but it took several meetings in various East Berlin cafés to convince them that I meant business. At these meetings I always made a point of paying for the drinks, taking care that my roll of notes should be seen, but of course paying only with the genuine money. Finally, it was agreed that 1,000 Bank of England £5 notes would be made ready for me within a week.

During the interval the German police, keeping me under observation, discovered that two of the four characters I had been dealing with had criminal records as coiners and passport forgers, and that all four left their homes early every morning and went to a house on the outskirts of Berlin. Eventually a raid was carried out and in the house were found paper and materials for making £5 notes. Several arrests were made and the men concerned were later convicted of forgery and sentenced to various terms of imprisonment.

When I returned my forged reichsmarks to Dr. Zauche, he told me that altogether 80,000 reichsmarks (at that time worth roughly £65,000) had been circulated in various German cities, but that in spite of all their inquiries the police had found no trace of the forgers. Recently, however, this flood of counterfeit notes seemed to have stopped. So far as I was concerned, that seemed to be the end of the matter.

Then in April 1938, the Bank of England sent to the Yard some forged £5 and £10 notes. Paper, watermarks, and printing were all excellent and no one but an expert could have told that anything was wrong with them. The only information the Bank had was that the notes had come from Paris.

I immediately went over there and saw Monsier Mondanel, Director General of the Sûreté. After explaining my mission and that we had no information whatever to work on, I suggested that with an inspector from the Sûreté I should go to all the places where it was likely that English bank notes might be changed or accepted in payment—banks, bureaux de change, tourist offices, the larger hotels, and so forth—and should show both the forgeries and some genuine notes to responsible officials and explain how to detect one from the other. I would also ask that if anyone presented a forged note he should be detained and the police sent for.

Ten tedious days were spent doing this. Everyone was naturally very interested and cooperative and assured me they would do as I asked. I saw Monsieur Mondanel again before I left for home and he promised that if anyone were detained, he would let the Yard know immediately.

When I reported back to the Yard, the authorities were not impressed by what I had done. Then about a fortnight later I saw in *Le Matin,* which I then used to read every day, that a man had been arrested in Paris for trying to change some forged English bank notes and that £5 and £10 notes to the face value of £475 had been found on him. Nothing had been heard from the Sûreté, but when I showed the report in *Le*

Matin to the Assistant Commissioner, I was directed to go to
Paris and find out what it was all about.

When I got there I was shown the notes which the police
had found and comparing them with those that the Bank of
England had sent to the Yard, I saw that they were identical
forgeries. I then asked to see the man who had been detained.
He had refused to say anything about himself to the French
police, and every tag or label on clothing by which he might
have been identified had been cut off. I started by questioning
him in French, but found he didn't speak it very well, so then
I tried German, and then Swedish, and then Danish, as he
looked as though he might have been a Scandinavian, but with
no result. (Later I learned that he was German, but spoke with
such a strong Württemberg accent that I could not understand
him.) However, he did seem to understand English, though he
spoke it with a strong accent. He denied ever having been to
England, but I knew he was lying because his talk was full of
the sort of colloquialisms that you can only pick up by living
in the country where they are in common use.

Although the French police had found nothing by which to
identify him, I decided to examine his clothes. On his shirt I
discovered a laundry mark—K 157. It was obvious from the
look of the figures that it was an English mark. At last I had
something positive to work on.

I returned to London with the man's photograph and fingerprints, but found there was no trace of him in our records;
so I sent a request to the CID at every police station in London
for inquiries to be made about the laundry mark at all laun-
dries in their districts. As I expected, scores of people living all
over London had the number K 157 allotted to them. I spent a
solid week going from one address to another, showing the
man's photograph and asking if anyone knew him by sight. At
the end of the week I had had no success, but there were still a
few people to call on. One of them, named Beckert, lived at 2A
Shoot-Up Hill, Cricklewood, in northwest London. When I
got there I found the house was empty with an agent's sign
saying it was TO LET. Alongside the front door was a name
plate inscribed F. Beckert—Photographer. I felt certain that at

last my long and weary journeys round Paris and London were nearing their end.

I went straight to the house agent, who to my joy identified the man in my photograph as Beckert. He was a German who had lived at No. 2A with his niece and had disappeared owing a considerable amount of rent. To recover what was owing the agent had put the bailiffs in and sold what was left of Beckert's property, which included cameras and other photographic materials. The agent said the house was empty, so I borrowed the keys and went back to Shoot-Up Hill to have a look round.

Except for the sort of litter you would expect in an empty house, I found nothing. I made an excuse to call on the good lady who lived next door and during a conversation with her I learned that Beckert's niece was called Beatrice, that she had a boyfriend who worked in a local garage, and that an odd-job man used to work in the house. My talkative informant even remembered his name, though not where he lived, except that it was at Burnt Oak, some five miles away. She told me also that two weeks earlier she had intended to have words with Beatrice about smoke and smuts that had poured one day from Beckert's chimney, ruining her washing which was hanging out in the garden. But Beatrice vanished before she could do so.

My next move was to trace the adddress of the odd-job man. This I did through the voters' list at the town hall, and that evening I went to see him. He told me he had worked for Beckert for some years and that from time to time bills for rent, gas, electricity, and so on had mounted up and that on these occasions Beckert used to lock himself up in the front room of the basement, sometimes for three or four days at a time, and would then emerge and go abroad for about a week. When he came back he would give the fellow money for his wages, if they were overdue, and to pay any outstanding bills.

What had been going on seemed pretty obvious; but one thing puzzled me. Beckert had apparently been carrying on in this way for the past five or six years, but the first forged English notes that had caused the present investigation to be made had been received by the Bank of England barely a month before.

I decided to have another look at the front basement room at No. 2A, as this had obviously been the scene of Beckert's operations, to see if there was anything I had overlooked on my first visit. So I borrowed the keys again and went down into the basement. There was nothing in it except a gas stove, an empty cupboard, and in the fireplace, standing on a concrete slab, one of those round iron stoves which the French call a *poêle* with a pipe going up the chimney.

I stood there imagining what I would have done if I had been in Beckert's shoes. Presumably in the process of printing the notes some of them would have been spoiled and these I would have scrunched up and thrown on the floor, and at the end of the day I would have swept them up in a heap towards the stove and burned them. Between the floorboards and the slab on which the stove was standing, I noticed a crack, so I decided to investigate. I borrowed a jimmy, then came back and pried up one of the boards in front of the slab. Groping about in the dust and dirt underneath, I found two photographic negatives. I cleaned them and held them up to the light: one showed a note for twenty reichsmarks, the other for fifty. I thought of the German notes I had seen and used in Berlin in 1935, and I decided to take up some more boards. Under the floor near the gas stove I found some broken and partly melted printing plates. Enough of them was left to show that some bore an impression of the watermark of a Bank of England note and others, to my surprise, the watermark of Belgian bank notes. I had heard nothing about any forged bank notes being in circulation.

My next call was at the Aliens Registration Office, where I got photographs of both Beckert and Beatrice. I then went back to Cricklewood and started a tour of the garages—there to try and trace Beatrice's boyfriend. After visiting several garages without result, I came across a young man who, when I said I had come to talk about Beatrice Beckert, denied that he knew her; but I could tell from his manner that he was lying. I had no proof, of course, but instinct counts almost as much as experience in deciding whether a suspect is speaking the truth.

The young man's father presently appeared and after I had told him who I was, his son admitted that he did know Beatrice and gradually we got him to reveal that she had gone to Brussels and was staying at 62 Rue de Brabant. He also admitted that Beatrice had left two suitcases for him to look after, which he produced and opened. One was full of ties bearing the names of shops all over Germany, the other contained scores of wallets—all obviously bought by Beckert in the course of changing his forged notes. Before I left, I warned the young man not to communicate with Beatrice or tell her about my inquiries.

My next step was to go to Brussels, where Monsieur Louwage, Chief of the *police judiciare*, was an old friend of mine. After I had told him my story, I showed him the plates of the Belgian bank notes. He almost hit the ceiling. He pressed all the buttons on his desk to bring his senior officers in and excitedly repeated what I had told him. Then I learned that for almost two years Belgium had been flooded with forged notes for 500 and 1,000 francs to the face value of 700,000 francs (approximately £24,000). The forgeries had been so good that they had remained undetected until they arrived at the Banque de Belgique. The Belgian police had made every effort to discover their origin, but without success.

I was anxious to see Beatrice, so an inspector was told to go with me. I wanted to take a taxi, but the inspector said it would be a waste of money; we could get to the Rue de Brabant by tram in fifteen minutes. However, I insisted on taking a taxi, and as we stopped at the house, a girl came out of the front door with two suitcases. I recognized her at once as Beatrice, from the photograph I had got from the Alien's Registration Office. We stopped her and explained who we were and took her back into the house. I asked her where she was going and she said to Germany, her homeland. I asked her why at this particular moment. She didn't answer. I began to search her handbag and in it found a telegram from her Cricklewood boyfriend telling her about my interview with him and that I was probably on my way to Brussels to see her. She admitted that the telegram had come within the last hour, but denied any knowledge of her uncle's whereabouts or of his forgeries, and she had left London two weeks before, after waiting without news of him for a month.

We took her to the Palais de Justice and there, after being questioned at some length, she broke down and told us her story. She insisted that she had had no idea about her uncle's activities until she had grown alarmed by his being away for two weeks—his trips abroad usually lasted only a few days—and needing some money to pay bills, she had searched for a key to the basement cupboard in case there might be some money there. She had eventually discovered a key, but no money. Instead, she found in the cupboard a number of spoiled forged English and Belgian bank notes and materials and apparatus for forging them. She immediately assumed that the reason she had heard nothing from her uncle was because he had been arrested somewhere. So she decided to burn all the paper and negatives (hence the smoke smuts that had spoiled the washing of the lady next door) and to try and destroy the plates, which she did partly by melting them on the gas ring and then breaking them, and had hidden the pieces by pushing them through holes in the floor. She had also found two suitcases which she had asked her boyfriend to look after until she returned from Brussels.

I now had enough evidence to get Beckert extradited from France to England. But Monsieur Louwage also had enough to get him extradited to Belgium and could set the wheels in motion at once. I could do nothing until I got back to London, and also I had to see Beckert on the way. Monsieur Louwage made me a sporting offer: as it was through me that Beckert had been traced, he would delay his request for extradition for seven days.

I went at once to Paris with a detective inspector from the Belgian police and again interviewed Beckert, who had been detained on a charge of attempted false pretences. In spite of what I was now able to tell him, he still denied his identity. I then told him casually that Beatrice had been detained by the police in Brussels. His manner changed immediately. He admitted that he was Beckert and said he would tell me everything if Beatrice were released. I told him I could promise nothing (in fact, no action was taken against her and a few weeks later the Belgian police let her go) but he decided to make a statement all the same. The gist of it was that he had been experimenting with color photography, but had found it so expensive that in order to keep going he had decided to forge reichsmark notes and cash them in West Germany by buying ties, shirts, and so on. But about 1934 or 1935 he noticed that shopkeepers were carefully examining the notes he gave them, so he started printing Belgian notes instead. Then in 1937 the same thing began to happen in Belgium, so at the beginning of 1938 he switched to printing English bank notes and cashing them in France.

Monsieur Louwage stuck to his agreement. I brought Beckert back to England with me and, in July 1938, he was charged on various counts at the Old Bailey. To all of them he pleaded guilty and was sentenced to four years' penal servitude.

This case had a curious aftermath. A report on it having been sent to the Berlin police, Dr. Zauche asked to be allowed to come over and interview Beckert. He arrived without warning in the middle of the Munich crisis and protested to my astonishment that he knew nothing of what was going on and everything was quiet in Berlin. I arranged to take him to Parkhurst Prison on the Isle of Wight to see Beckert the next morning, but as we were on the way to the station he saw air-raid shelters being built in St. James' Park and other warlike preparations being made. He decided that he wanted to go home at once. I persuaded him to stay on condition that we should not speak during the journey, as we would have had to converse in German.

After he had interviewed Beckert we returned to London and I arranged to meet him at his hotel at ten o'clock the next morning. But at 6 A.M. he telephoned to say that he had decided to catch the eight o'clock boat train for Harwich and nothing I could say would dissuade him from going. He later wrote to say that the German authorities would apply for Beckert's extradition at the end of his sentence. He need not have bothered. At the end of it Beckert was interned and after the War he was deported.

Conspiracy

(7)

☞ I have to confess that I have seldom read detective stories. Often they are technically inaccurate and equally often are psychologically farfetched. But my distrust of them lies mainly in the inherent improbability of the sort of events with which so many of them seem to deal. To anyone with a knowledge of police work, not to mention some understanding of human behavior, such events invalidate the motives and procedures which the author ascribes to the detective—when he is a detective and not an archaeologist, a don, a journalist, or some other type of enthusiastic amateur gifted with second-sight and a taste for crime. Only very occasionally have I come across a case that might justifiably be said to show that truth *is* sometimes stranger than fiction.

An investigation that I had to make in 1938 may be said, I think, to fall into this category. The more I found out about the affair, the more improbable did it seem to become, and if it was less sinister or less violent than a good many detective stories, it outdid any that I have read in its calculated and ruthless ingenuity.

The matter came to the attention of the police when a firm of London solicitors asked the Yard to investigate the affairs of a client of theirs whom they believed was being swindled. The persons chiefly concerned were the client, a young Scotsman, whom I will call John; Mary, a woman with whom he became friendly; Richard, her husband; and Judy, who intermittently was Richard's mistress. Until John's solicitors approached the Yard, nothing about the matter was known to the police and it was a long and extremely difficult job piecing together the various fragments of the story. As things turned out, it was also an unrewarding one, in spite of the painstaking accumulation of a very large dossier.

John, who was the only son of a well-to-do father, was born in 1903. He left school in Edinburgh in 1920, his father having died a year before, and for the next two years he was tutored by two clergymen. In 1926 his mother died and he succeeded to the family estates. (He was, incidentally, also the heir of his uncle, a rich man with a title.) Administration of the estate was granted to a number of trustees, possibly because John's father had been understandably anxious about his ability to handle matters of business. His mother, too, had been sufficiently worried about him to have him mentally examined, and though it was decided that he was not actually insane, his intellectual development was undoubtedly below average.

After his mother's death John continued to live in the house where he had spent all his life, but he was lonely and without any friends. He felt the lack of society, especially that of women, and in an attempt to form acquaintance he wrote to a correspondence club in London. As a result, he was put in touch with several young women, but none of them appealed to him until he discovered Mary, who wrote to him in the middle of 1927. She described herself as a governess and said she was living in lodgings in Edinburgh. When they met she struck him as a cheerful, intelligent sort of girl and before long they became close friends. John soon began to confide in her and though in course of time they became intimate in the things they talked about, there was never any question of a physical relationship. (When I interviewed John in 1938 he told me he had never had sexual intercourse, which I could well believe.)

Early in 1938, Mary had asked John to help her, as she had lost her job, or so she said, and from time to time he gave her sums of money. For several months they went about together, to dancing classes and to the seaside, where on one occasion she persuaded him to photograph her naked. Soon after this she introduced him to a man to whom she said she was engaged. This was Richard, and within a month she told John that they had got married. However, soon afterwards she said that Richard had left her and that she was again in need of money, which, as before, John gave her.

At the beginning of 1929 the two of them left Edinburgh and came to England, where they stayed at various places on the south coast, always in separate establishments, but with John visiting Mary every day. (The purpose of this arrangement, so far as I could discover, was to avoid giving an impression that Mary had any sort of influence over John.) In this way, traveling about from place to place, though with Mary ostensibly independent of him, they lived for the next five years, during which John continued to foot the bill. His annual income at this time was about £1,000, derived from investments, and there is no doubt that he spent every penny of it.

At the end of a year or so there was not much that Mary did not know about John's character, about his weaknesses and his foibles, and about his family history. She had also found out that jewelry and silver that he had inherited from his mother was stored in a bank in Edinburgh. At the beginning of 1934 she told him she had discovered that some relatives of his had been to the bank and had managed to take away some of the silver. (Although there was not a grain of truth in this, John believed her.) She suggested that they should go to Edinburgh and remove the remaining valuables from the bank, so that she could keep them in safety. John, apparently without question, agreed to this, so they went to Scotland and withdrew from the bank a chest containing the family silver and jewelry, which John handed over to Mary. It was the last he ever saw of the chest or its contents.

Two months later Mary told him that she found out that some of his relatives were having him watched by detectives and that a cousin had called at the address where he was now staying, at Worthing in Sussex, in order to make inquiries about him. The intention, she said, was obvious: it was to have him certified and sent to an asylum. Her objective this time was apparently to create in John feelings of apprehension and persecution which she intended to exploit later on.

A month afterwards she told John that she wanted to exchange her car for a new one and needed £175 to complete the deal. This was the start of a maneuver that might well have bewildered someone considerably less stupid than John. From his bank in Hove he drew £175 in cash which he gave to Mary, but instead of completing the purchase of the car, she asked him to put the money in a suitcase, together with his camera, and then to leave the case in the cloakroom at Hove station. A day or so later, accompanied by Mary, he withdrew the case and went with her to London, this time leaving the case in the luggage office at Victoria.

A few days later, Mary, in a state of some concern, handed him his camera, which she said someone had sent her through the post. It was obvious in her view that whoever had done so must have induced the attendant at Hove station to release the case and must also have had a duplicate key for it, as she still had her own key and the cloakroom ticket. She suggested she should ask Richard (of whom John had heard no mention since his apparent abandonment of Mary) to collect the case and return it to her. The next day she told John this had been done and that Richard, on opening the case (how he was able to do so without a key she didn't explain) had found it to be full of stones. Not only was John's camera missing, but also the £175 in notes. It is an indication of John's mental state that he not only accepted this farrago of rubbish without making any inquiries of the police or the railway authorities, but drew another £175 from his bank to replace the missing money.

Mary was now frequently traveling to London first class, staying in expensive hotels, and going to smart restaurants, all at John's expense. On the occasions when he went too, he traveled separately, third class, stayed in bed-and-breakfast lodgings, and contented himself with eating in cheap cafés. This was not due to parsimony. In fact, it showed a glimmer of good sense, for in order to keep pace with Mary's style of living John had by this time incurred an overdraft of £7,800.

By now he was so completely dominated by Mary and Richard that they had no difficulty in getting him to accept anything they told him, no matter how foolish or fantastic it might appear to be, and to act in whatever way they suggested. By various tricks and stories they preyed on his natural apprehensions, causing him to doubt not only the evidence of his own senses, but also the motives and conduct of other people. On one occasion Mary handed him a small parcel which she said an unknown girl had given her as a present for him. In it was a watch that he recognized as one that he had left in a jewel case with some other valuables at his bank in London. It did not occur to him at the time that Mary had had the case in her possession the day before he left it at the bank, the safety and integrity of which he now began to doubt.

In September 1934, Mary told him she thought it would be a good thing to engage some "watchers" to keep observation on the detectives whom his relations were employing to shadow him. She need £500 to pay them and asked him to let her have it in £1 notes. (Notes of higher denomination, as no doubt she well knew, might have been more easily traced.) With this profitable story she continued to mulct John for some time. Later he gave her another £500 and before this particular gambit gave out he had parted with a total of £4,500 drawn from various bank accounts in England and Scotland.

Eventually his trustees began to object to his making fresh inroads on his capital, but Mary was not to be deterred. At her dictation he wrote to the trustees asking them to pay her

£1,000 in settlement of two IOU's for £500 each, which he had given her. The letter claimed that this money had been spent in trying to trace some illegitimate half-caste children of his father's, the result of his cohabitation with a woman in Malaya, where he lived for many years. John had told Mary of this mottled page in his family's history—whether it was true or not, he did not know—and she seized on it as a means of frightening the trustees into acquiescence, guessing, rightly, that they would probably prefer to pay the money than risk a scandal. It is hardly necessary to add that not a penny had been spent in the way described in the letter, nor that John had not borrowed any money from Mary. Nevertheless the bogus IOUs were sent to the trustees, in return for which the £1,000 was duly paid.

Throughout 1935 the incongruous association between the two persisted, with Mary now living in a flat in Park Lane and John continuing to make her substantial payments, supposedly intended for the "watchers" that she said were still being employed.

At the beginning of 1936 a letter arrived from the trustees which alarmed John considerably. It said that application was being made for a court order under which it would be possible to have him medically examined with a view to it being decided whether or not he was capable of managing his own affairs. If he would agree to the examination and it should be found to be favorable, his further requests for money would be acceded to. If not, the court would be asked to appoint a nominee. This letter tended not only to confirm the fears already implanted in his mind by Mary, that his relatives wanted to have him put away, but to make it seem that they also wanted to get their hands on his money.

It was not difficult for Mary to persuade him to refuse to be examined. In the hope of forestalling further moves she herself called in several doctors to get their opinion on his state of mind. However, they refused to commit themeslves, which was not much better than their giving an adverse report. So Mary decided to go a step further and a solicitor was instructed to apply to the Court of Session in Edinburgh for the appointment on John's behalf of a *curator bonis,* a term applicable in Scotland to one who is officially appointed as the custodian of the estate of one who is unfit to manage his own affairs.

In the meantime John was served with the order granted to the trustees. But Mary was still one jump ahead. She had been to see another solicitor, who had told her that if John were to acquire a wife this would automatically mean the suspension of the order. Richard, who now appeared on the scene once more, said that if John would agree to marry, he would find him a bride. John's apprehension and perplexity by this time can well be imagined. There seemed to be nothing to do but consent, and he did so. That evening Richard left to find the bride for John and to get a special license.

The next day Mary brought John to the church, where on the steps he met his bride for the first time and the ceremony was performed with two taxi drivers as witnesses. As soon as it was over his wife left, not with him, but with Richard and a woman who had come to the church with her. It may seem difficult to credit it, but John failed to notice an important fact about his bride: she was in an advanced state of pregnancy. (The woman who accompanied her was, in fact, a midwife.) She herself was a girl called Judy and was the mistress of Richard, the father of her child, who was born a week later. With an eye to future operations against the guileless and pathetic John, the child, unknown to him, was registered as being his and consequently given his name.

Here let me give a word of explanation about the apparent ease with which Richard had contrived to produce Judy at the critical moment. They had first met in 1932, and in 1935 Judy, finding herself pregnant and having no idea that Richard was a married man (or, for that matter, that his name was not what he said it was), agreed to marry him. Wishing no doubt to keep her as far away from his wife as possible, Richard rented a furnished bungalow for Judy near Padstow in Cornwall. Early in March 1936, he went down to see her and told her a strange and plausible story which she nevertheless accepted. He asked if she would help him by marrying a friend

of his whose uncle was trying to get him certified as a lunatic
to prevent him inheriting some money, and was also threatening to take legal proceedings against Richard himself. If his
friend were to get married this would cause his certification
and the proceedings against himself to be withdrawn. Judy, he
said, would easily be able to get a divorce later on.

She, poor girl, was in a desperate situation. Her child was
due within a few days and she was afraid that if she refused to
do what Richard asked, he would desert her. (She still did not
know, of course, that he was married.) And so she had agreed
to go through with the ceremony.

Richard's next move was to present her with a draft letter
to an Edinburgh solicitor asking him to oppose on her behalf
the appointment of a *curator bonis* and saying that it was she
who had been responsible for John's reckless expenditure. After
some persuasion she copied out the letter and sent it off.

As Mary's solicitor had predicted, the application by John's
trustees for an order for his compulsory examination immediately became ineffective on his marriage and the trustees were
compelled to hand over to him all the money and securities in
their possession.

In June 1936 the two of them explained their new scheme.
Richard suggested to John that it was time he made provision
for his wife and child. He said he knew of a public house in the
west of England which would be a good investment for the
future. The price was £2,575, and very soon a check for this
amount, payable to his wife, had been made out by John and
handed to Richard. This Richard persuaded Judy to endorse
and with the money he bought the public house, intending it,
in his own words, as a home for her child and herself. The
license was to belong to a Mrs. M., for whom Richard had been
working, he himself would be the manager, and Judy the bar-
maid. For a short while all apparently went well, but before
long rows developed between the three of them, which ended
in Judy being pressured into going away to stay with her
parents. In April 1937 Richard told her that he had sold the
pub and given the money back to John (who, in fact, got not

so much as a farthing). He begged her to live with him again, but she refused to do so. In August she gave birth to a second child, of whom Richard was the father.

Mary now suggested to John that he should open a bank account in London in which to place his assets. Accordingly, John did so, but in a little over three months £2,000 was drawn out, and in the following month, July, a further £1,000. Altogether more than £7,000 was drawn from the account in about fifteen months, the procedure always being the same as it had been when John banked at Hove. The amount was drawn out by him in £1 notes and handed to Mary, who waited outside in a taxi. Never once was she seen by any of the bank staff. From various sums that John handed over to her in this way she usually returned to him £3 or £4.

Towards the end of March 1937, Mary, finding she was pregnant, went to a doctor in Harley Street. The tale she told him was even more incredible than any of her others. She explained that three and a half months earlier, in December 1936, while she was traveling by car in Cornwall with her husband, she had given birth to a son, whose arrival had been duly recorded at the local registry. The child, she said, was fit and well and she had not thought it necessary to see a doctor. So impressed by the details of her story was the doctor whom she had gone to consult that he had her examined by four leading obstetricians, who confirmed that she was well advanced in pregnancy. At the end of March a daughter was born. Although the doctor, whom I later interviewed, denied that he had believed Mary's story of a "delayed twin," and considered that she was a pathological liar, he had nevertheless been sufficiently impressed at the time to write a article in a medical journal, of which the heading was "Does Superfetation Occur?—Report of a possible case"—something of a tribute to the conviction with which Mary must have told her tale.

The purpose of all this I never understood, unless it was that at the back of her mind she had some idea of insuring against the possibility of a hitch occurring in establishing Judy's child as John's heir, and that a substitute should be provided in case of need; though how this plan, if that was what was in her mind, would have been brought into operation, I do not know.

By this time Mary had got effective control of all John's assets and she forced him to sell securities amounting to several thousand pounds. Although this was done quite legally through a solicitor, Mary was careful that no documents concerning the transaction got into John's hands. Similarly, her next move, the transfer of his house in Edinburgh to herself and its conversion into maisonettes, was on the face of it legally executed, though John was shown none of the documents, except for the purpose of putting his signature to them.

By now, all his unsettled money in various bank accounts, amounting to almost £15,000, and all his investments and property had passed into Mary's hands or been transferred to her. She had induced him also to agree to her becoming the beneficiary of a will under which he would have received £1,000 on the death of his aunt. This was Mary's final fling. Satisfied that there was nothing more to be got out of their association, she seized the first opportunity to pick a quarrel with John and threw him out of the house, penniless, friendless, and with not a shred of proof of the manner in which he had been cheated.

There is reason to believe that second thoughts may have suggested to Mary that there might be a hope that at some distant time in the future something more might be squeezed out of her victim. A series of fantastically complicated maneuvers involving Judy and her two children, the false registration of the child Mary claimed to have had in December 1936, the actual birth, an unsuccessful prosecution of Richard for receiving a child, threats, subterfuge and lies—all these and a number of related incidents pointed strongly to the existence of a scheme in Mary's mind whereby she might one day have profited from the legal recognition that one of the children involved was John's heir and would eventually inherit the estate of John's rich uncle. Fortunately such recognition, which could only have been got by false pretences, was never given.

In all this conglomeration of lies and misrepresentation we could find nothing, thanks to Mary's thoroughness and ingenuity, on which to base a prosecution with any hope of its being successful. She and Richard between them had taken good care to prevent anything in the way of documentary evidence about their activities being retained by John, so that virtually there was nothing to go on except his word; and it was not difficult to imagine the sort of figure he would have cut in the witness box under incisive cross-examination.

With some people who are the victims of a fraud or a confidence trick you feel that really they have only themselves to blame, that greed or self-esteem, or perhaps even sheer carelessness, has landed them in trouble. It was impossible to feel this in John's case, even though stupidity was obviously the cause of his ruin. But it was the stupidity of someone mentally below the average, whose dull-wittedness and inexperience had been cruelly exploited. He was, when I first saw him, thirty-five years old. He was not what could have been described as a mental case, but he was extremely vague and disjointed in his conversation. By dealing with him gently and with the utmost patience—I could only question him for three or four hours a day at the most—I was gradually able to piece his story together and to get enough information out of him to start making inquiries; though, as I say, none of these yielded sufficient information to provide a water-tight case. It seemed at various times that charges of false pretences, of fraudulent conversion, and of incitement to commit perjury might be possible, but each time on closer examination the evidence turned out to be too flimsy for the police to risk a prosecution.

Perhaps the worst injustice of this truly pathetic case was that in 1938 Judy, abandoned by Richard, summoned John for failing to maintain her and her two children and an order was made against him for payment to her of £2 a week.

As a detective one tries not to feel vindictive about the criminals with whom one has to deal. For a few of them one can even feel some sort of sympathy. A man or a woman driven to distraction by the most contemptible of all crimes, blackmail, may see no deliverance from the clutches of his persecutor except by stealing or embezzlement. The deceived or discarded lover who commits a *crime passionnel* may have been so treated as to make the offence seem understandable in the circumstances. The childless woman who abducts a baby with no thought of bringing it to any harm, indeed with the reverse intention, is not simply to be condemned, whatever the distress she may have caused. She must surely be pitied also. But in the case of such ruthless and calculating predators as Mary and her husband, battening on a creature so defenseless as John, it is difficult not to feel disappointed that they were not brought to justice.

The Penn Murder
(8)

To anyone familiar with police procedure, accounts in newspapers and novels of the way criminal investigations are conducted usually show very little knowledge of what really happens. They give no inkling as a rule of the system, thoroughness, patience, and accuracy of observation that are indispensable to the solving of most crimes, or of the cooperation, which is often equally essential, of authorities such as the local police, pathologists, coroners, and others. Last but not least, a small percentage of luck enters into the solution of a good many crimes. Although it occurred close on thirty years ago, since when scientific aids to detection have been enormously improved, the case of Harold Hill, a soldier, who murdered two small girls in 1941, still exemplifies the sort of procedure that is followed in a murder inquiry that starts from scratch; that is to say, with nothing whatever to go on except the existence of the corpse to prove that a crime has been committed. This crime was not in fact a very difficult one to solve, but it may be of interest to see exactly how each of the factors I have mentioned came into play, even including that small percentage of luck.

At three-thirty on Wednesday, November 19, 1941, in the Buckinghamshire village of Penn, two small girls, Doreen Hearne, aged eight, and Kathleen Trendle, aged six, came out of school and set off for their homes in the village about half a mile away. At a crossroad near their homes they saw an army lorry. The two girls asked the driver for a ride. Some other children heard him tell the girls to get in and off they went. When they failed to arrive home, their parents began to feel alarmed. Hearing that they had gone for a ride with a soldier, they decided to tell the police and inquiries were started.

The next day the girls were still missing and searches were organized by the police, helped by villagers, and Boy Scouts. Three days later the girls' bodies were found in a copse called Rough Wood, about four miles from the village. Both girls had been stabbed several times in the throat. There had been very heavy rain almost every day since the beginning of the month and it was obvious from the dampness of their clothing and the dryness of the ground under their bodies that they had been lying there since the evening of the day they disappeared.

The bodies were discovered on November 22. At ten o'clock that night I was told that the Buckinghamshire police had asked Scotland Yard for help and that I was to take charge of the case. I telephoned at once to say that I was coming down and that meanwhile nothing at the scene of the crime was to be touched. The local police had no information to give me, except that the girls' bodies had been removed from the copse where they were found to the mortuary.

At seven o'clock the next morning Sir Bernard Spilsbury, the pathologist, and a junior officer who was to assist me arrived at my house and we set off by car for the Bucks police headquarters at Chesham.

The local inspector repeated to us the few facts that were known and said that since inquiries had begun they had come across various people who had seen a military lorry traveling along some of the local roads with two little girls sitting in front with the driver.

We were then taken to the wood where the bodies had been found, which was about six miles away. It is often useful for the pathologist working on a case of this sort to have a look at the scene for himself, so as to see the exact state of the ground, the position of the body when found in relation to various objects, and so on. So although the bodies had been removed, Sir Bernard Spilsbury came with us.

The local police had carried out very carefully my instructions that nothing was to be disturbed. We went along a wide path through the wood to a spot eighty-one feet from the south edge of the path, where the body of Doreen, the elder girl, had been found. Sixty-six and a half feet from the other side of the path Kathleen's body had been found. Both girls had had their clothing up under their arms, but their underclothes had not been interfered with. Doreen's left shoe had been found lying near her feet and her overcoat rolled up on the ground near her stomach. Kathleen's left shoe and stocking were both missing. In spite of the girls' injuries there were no bloodstains on the ground where their bodies had been lying. Before they were taken to the mortuary they had both been photographed in the positions in which they had been discovered.

I made a search of the area and twenty-six feet from where Kathleen's body had been found there was a khaki handkerchief. On it was a laundry mark, RA 1019. Fifty-six feet from where Doreen had been found a fawn sock, later identified as Kathleen's, was hanging on the branch of a fir tree about four feet from the ground. We also found her red leather gas-mask case and four feet farther on her missing shoe. Later, a hair ribbon found on the north edge of the path was identified as Doreen's.

Because of the heavy rain the path through the wood was fairly soft. Deep tire marks showed that a motor vehicle of some sort had been driven along it. You could see that after going a certain distance it had turned round, crushing the growth on both sides of the path, and had then gone a little way back and stopped at a point roughly half-way between the two bodies. The tire marks were deeper at this spot and quite a large area was stained with oil. It was obvious that this was where the vehicle had stopped while the murderer got rid of the bodies and that it had stood there for some minutes. It was equally obvious that it must have had a bad oil leak, which I concluded was either from the back axle or one of the back wheels.

A little to the east of this spot, eight feet from the path, I found a patch of ground stained with blood and another patch four feet farther on. Two feet beyond this there was a blood-stained leaf. These stains suggested to me that the murderer had paused while he was carrying the bodies from the vehicle to the place where he had left them and that while he paused he had dumped the bodies on the ground.

A very careful search was made of the whole area, but nothing else of significance was found. Where the various articles had been discovered and the movements of the vehicle could be seen I placed markers and then arranged for photographs to be taken in case later on I should need to refer to the position of anything that had been discovered. I also asked for plaster casts to be made of the tire marks and had a good solid chunk, about a spit deep, of the oil-stained earth taken up and sent off for chemical analysis.

Taking with us all the articles we had found, we went on to the mortuary, where I watched Sir Bernard Spilsbury perform postmortems on the two bodies. The elder girl, Doreen, had three wounds in the neck, one of them a large wound which looked as though the weapon had probably been turned round in it. She also had six small puncture wounds in the chest, three of which had penetrated to the lung, and a fourth which had fractured the third left rib. Her clothes were soaked with blood and rain and infested with insects, but there was nothing to suggest any sexual interference.

Kathleen had eleven stab wounds in the throat, each about five-eighths of an inch wide. One had penetrated to her spinal column. Her clothing was in the same state as Doreen's and as in her case there were no signs of sexual interference. The

importance of examining the exact nature of the wounds was
to find out, if possible, what type of weapon had been used.
Sir Bernard said he thought that the same one had been used
in each case, that it had a blunt point and a rather blunt single
cutting edge and was five-eighths of an inch wide.

He also said that it looked as though both girls had been
partially strangled before being stabbed and that they had died
slowly, the cause of death being hemorrhage from the stab
wounds. Doreen had lost anything up to six pints of blood and
Kathleen anything up to four. Samples of their blood were
taken and sent to the laboratory for grouping, and I took some
hair from both their heads. The purpose of this was in case we
should need to make comparisons later on.

The contents of Doreen's stomach included some partly
digested food resembling potato, with some green vegetables
and a little meat and fat. Similar food was found in the upper
part of the small intestine. The contents of Kathleen's stomach
were much the same, but included more potato and no green
vegetable.

I saw the parents of the dead girls. Mrs. Hearne told me
that for her midday meal on the day she disappeared Doreen
had had meat pie, potatoes, cabbage, and apple pie with
custard. She had left home to return to school at 12:50. The
clothes she had been wearing were the same as those she had
on when her body was found, and she had been carrying her
gas-mask in a black tin can.

Mrs. Trendle said that for her lunch Kathleen had had only
minced beef and mashed potatoes. Her clothes, too, were the
same as those she was wearing when her body was found. She
had left to return to school just before one o'clock.

Sir Bernard's description of the stomach contents and the
position that the food had reached in the intestines, taken with
what we had learned from the two mothers, established beyond all question that the girls had been killed on the afternoon that they were taken away.

It will be remembered that no blood stains were found at the
place where the bodies were discovered, although the postmortem showed that both girls had lost large quantities of

blood. It was obvious therefore the girls must have been killed elsewhere, so it was arranged for an organized search to be made of the wood and of nearby coppices and open spaces to see if any spot could be found which was heavily stained with blood. The search parties were also told to look out for the black tin case containing Doreen's gas-mask. They were warned that if it was found it was not to be touched as it might have fingerprints on it.

The next thing to do was to interview the children who had last seen the two girls. Among a large number of children who were interviewed were three schoolgirls, all of them aged eleven, who had seen Doreen and Kathleen speaking to the lorry driver at the crossroad. Edward Page, a boy aged twelve, had cycled past the lorry while it was standing there, and another boy, aged ten, had walked past it. It is interesting that although the girls gave us a good description of the driver, they could not describe the lorry very well, whereas the boys, though not able to say what the driver looked like, except that he was a soldier, gave us a detailed description of the lorry.

We learned from the girls that the driver was about twenty-six, had "medium colored" hair and a reddish complexion and was wearing steel-rimmed glasses and a service cap. From the boys we learned that the lorry was a 15 cwt Fordson camouflaged to look like a wireless truck, but without an aerial, and that it had a canvas hood which was lower than the top of the driver's cabin. (This was interesting because the hood on this type of vehicle is always higher than the cabin and it suggested that in this case the hood had been improvised, as was proved when the lorry was finally traced.) The driver's cabin had steel doors, but no windows or weather shield. On the nearside front mudguard the figure 43 was painted in white on a red-and-blue square and on the offside front mudguard were the letters JP in blue, joined together on a red circle. Page, the twelve-year-old boy, added that in the radiator mesh towards the top right-hand corner was a Remembrance Day poppy. He also mentioned that there was a figure 5 on the offside front lamp.

Late that evening we had inquiries made at the War Office to find out which artillery unit used the markings described by the boys. We were told they belonged to the 86th Field Regiment of Royal Artillery and that this particular unit had been in the west country up to November 16, when it moved by stages to the east coast. From November 18 to 21 it had been at Haslemere in Bucks, a few miles from Rough Wood where the girls' bodies had been found, and had then moved on to Yoxford in Suffolk.

That night I sent to Scotland Yard and all Home Counties' forces a request for inquiries to be made at every laundry in their areas to find out to whom was allocated the laundry mark on the handkerchief picked up in the wood.

Two things that I found out later that evening were that steel-rimmed spectacles were an official issue to men in the forces and that the blade of an office-issue army knife was five-eighths of an inch wide. By this time it was close on midnight and that ended our labors for the day.

The next day we concentrated on inquiries throughout the roads and lanes between Penn and Rough Wood. We found quite a number of people who had seen the lorry with the girls sitting beside the driver on the day they had disappeared. As a result of our inquiries we were finally able to pinpoint the lorry's route from the time it left the crossroad to within a mile of the wood. As the point where it was last seen was on the main road leading to the wood, I felt pretty sure that we had established the complete route.

I now decided to go over this route myself in a police car from the crossroad to the middle of the wood where the oil-stained earth had been found. From this point we traveled by the most direct route to Haslemere where the artillery unit had camped, and then back to the crossroad again, driving as directly as possible. The speedometer showed the total distance to be fourteen miles. From this checking of the mileage there developed later the percentage of luck that I mentioned at the beginning.

It was now Monday night. I felt there was nothing more to be done in the area, so I decided to go to Yoxford the next morning. Before I left I arranged for a local surveyor to make two scale maps, one showing the school, the crossroad, and the route which we knew the lorry to have taken, the other of Rough Wood, showing the exact positions of the various objects we had found. This was in case it might be necessary to refer to these details later, perhaps to point them out to a judge or jury.

The searchers in the wood had so far found nothing, but late that night it was reported that the laundry mark had been identified: RA 1019 was that of the Royal Standard Laundry at Chiswick in London, and was allotted to a Harold Hill, who was in the Army.

When I arrived at Yoxford I saw the colonel of the regiment and told him the details of the murder and what our inquiries had established. He sent for his four battery commanders and after I had repeated the story one of them told me that a lorry in his battery was giving trouble and had a bad oil leak from the rear axle.

The driver of the lorry was a man named Hill. Except that the officer described him as wearing tortoise-shell glasses, his appearance fitted the description I had already got. The lorry was now in a barn some five miles away. We went there to see it and looking underneath I saw that there was a large patch of oil near the back nearside wheel.

We searched the lorry and pulled out a tarpaulin. On it were some large reddish-black stains which, after making an elementary test, I was satisfied were blood stains. Looking at the lorry as I walked around it, I was astonished at the accuracy of the twelve-year-old Edward Page's observation: his description was complete in every detail, down to the unit number and the poppy in the radiator. I examined the inside of the lorry, but could see no blood stains, and then took a sample of oil for analysis. Then I compared the casts of the tires which I had brought with me: they fitted exactly.

I now asked to see Hill. When he was brought in I told him I was investigating a murder and wanted to examine his belongings. There was nothing suspicious about the uniform he was wearing, but in his kit bag was a spare uniform which was very damp. Hill explained this by saying he had been out in the rain, but the trouser pockets and the lining of the tunic were far too damp for this to have been caused by rain. I concluded that the uniform had been soaked in water. On the back and front of the spare tunic, on the sleeves, and also on the trousers were some spots that looked like blood—spots such as I would have expected to find if a man had carried a badly bleeding child over his shoulder for some distance. Some shirts and handkerchiefs in the kit bag had the laundry mark RA 1019, but there was no knife in it, nor was there a pair of spectacles. (Hill, as his commanding officer had said, was wearing tortoise-shell glasses.)

It was at this point that the small percentage of luck crept in. All army drivers have to keep a log book in which they have to enter their vehicle's speedometer reading at the beginning and end of each day and the journeys made and their separate mileages. It had happened quite by accident that the battery commander had inspected his men's log books at Haslemere on November 20. The entry showing Hill's speedometer readings from the previous day, the day of the murders, recorded 4,420 miles at the beginning and 4,429 miles at the end of the day. Yet his speedometer reading when the check was made next day showed 4,472. Hill had made an authorized journey of nine miles on November 19 and on the next day two authorized journeys totaling twenty-nine miles in all. He could not account for the extra fourteen miles.

I asked Hill to accompany me to the local police station—he could of course have refused, as no charge had been made against him, but no doubt he assumed that this would have increased our suspicions—and I asked him to give a full account of what he did on November 19. He made a long statement, partly in answer to questions that I put to him, which I took down in writing.

The greater part of this statement was about routine duties, but two or three things proved to be of interest. After describing how he had spent the earlier part of the day, he said that he went into the mess for tea, where he had sausages and mash. He had seen no one that he knew in the mess. When I asked what his laundry mark was, he was very evasive and only admitted it was RA 1019 when shown his towel. He could not account for his marked handkerchief being found in the wood near the girls' bodies. All he would say was that it must have been returned in someone's else's laundry. When I asked about his knife, he said that he had lost it about four months earlier. The reason for my interest was that the width of the Army-issue knife blade corresponded to the width of the knife that Sir Bernard Spilsbury said had been used.

When I showed him the stains on the tarpaulin he looked at them in silence for some moments, then said, "It looks like blood." He stared at the tarpaulin for some time then suddenly said, "I don't admit that it's mine."

At this point I asked him to take off his tunic and saw that the sleeves of his shirt had been torn off at the elbow. His story was that they had been torn at the laundry in September and he had decided to shorten them for next summer. Remembering the bloodstains on the sleeves of his spare tunic, the one in the kit bag, it seemed pretty obvious that there might be a good reason for him to have cut off the sleeves of his shirt. Referring to his knife, he said, "I lost it some months ago and since have never had occasion to want one." He also said that about two months before he had reported the loss of two handkerchiefs to the quartermaster's stores. After he had read and signed his statement, we took possession of all the clothes he was wearing, then handed him back to the military.

We next took statements from some of the officers and men of Hill's battery about the speedometer readings and the oil leak, and also learned that when he joined the regiment Hill had been issued a pair of steel-rimmed glasses which he had worn until a few days earlier.

The next day I decided to return to London and took with me the lorry, the tarpaulin, and Hill's kit and clothing. When I arrived at my office I found that Doreen's gas-mask case had been found and sent to the Yard where it had been examined for fingerprints. Only a small part of one print could be found but this was sufficient to identify it as Hill's, that identification being made by checking the print with the files which showed that Hill had twice been convicted for indecent assault.

Hill's blood-stained clothing and the tarpaulins were sent

immediately to the laboratory for examination and the oil sample taken from his lorry to the chemist who had analyzed the oil-stained earth taken from Rough Wood. The lorry was also sent for examination.

The next day I received the results of these examinations. The blood on the tarpaulin was of the same group as that of the two girls. Some hairs which had also been found were similar to the hairs I had taken when the bodies were at the mortuary. The blood on the tunic and trousers found in Hill's kit bag was human blood, as were some spots that had been found in the lorry, but none of them could be grouped. It was also confirmed that the oil samples from the spit of earth and from Hill's lorry were of the same grade and quality.

I now felt that I had enough evidence on which to charge Hill with the murders, so the next day I went back to Yoxford and arrested him. He was taken to Chesham where he was charged and after appearing before the local court was remanded in custody for two weeks.

But that was by no means the end of the inquiry. There was still a lot to be done. What looks like a cast-iron case may sometimes be found to have a hole in it through some small but vital piece of evidence having escaped notice. I went back to Yoxford and began to take a number of statements from some of the officers and men in Hill's battery about his movements, his long journeys, and his account of his doings before and during the period covered by the disappearance of the girls and the discovery of their bodies.

The regimental medical officer said that Hill, whom he knew, had never at any time reported sick or had an injury that had caused hemorrhage.

At no time, according to the quartermaster sergeant and his staff, had Hill reported the loss of any handkerchiefs.

All the men in the battery confirmed that up to the morning of November 20 (the day after the murder) he had always worn steel-rimmed spectacles, but thereafter had worn a tortoise-shell pair.

The men who slept on either side of his bed were both quite definite that up to and including the night of November 8 the sleeves of Hill's shirt were not torn. One went so far as to say that he had noticed on the morning of the twentieth that Hill had shortened them.

Two men of the Battery had borrowed Hill's knife (which he claimed to have lost four months earlier), at the end of October and several times later on, they having lost theirs.

Checking on the meals served on November 19, I found that no sausages and mash had been served for tea on that date (as Hill had claimed), nor for some days before or afterwards. Not one of all the men in the Battery who went in to tea that day could remember having seen Hill at tea time.

After I had taken all these statements, many of them corroborating each other, I prepared a report for the Director of Public Prosecutions which was submitted with all the statements, photographs, and plans that had been accumulated during the course of the inquiry.

Hill's trial, at which he pleaded not guilty, took place at the end of January and lasted four days. His counsel first tried to prove that the long statement which I had taken down from Hill was true. Then he pleaded that Hill was a schizophrenic and that if he did commit the murders, he did not know what he was doing. The jury returned a verdict of guilty and he was sentenced to death. Later he appealed, but his appeal was dismissed and in April 1942 he was hanged.

Not, as I have said, a very difficult case to solve, but one that might have been much more difficult to prove if experience had not taught me the importance of always being strictly methodical in carrying out an investigation, and of overlooking no detail that might seem to have a bearing on the case, however insignificant it may appear to be at first sight.

In Confidence
(9)

☞ Whatever other factors may play a part periodically in reducing certain types of crime, I am convinced that there is no stronger deterrent than the certainty of conviction. Proof of this is shown by the marked decline of the confidence trickster, a species of criminal almost unknown nowadays, who more or less disappeared from the scene following a change of policy in the late 1930s. The con man's victims were always people living abroad (the farther away the better) for without the evidence of his victim, as the trickster well knew, there was no danger of prosecution. Few visitors from Australia, the American Middle West, or elsewhere, having been fleeced during a trip to London, were prepared to return simply in order to give the police a helping hand in their investigations. Having reported the circumstances of their loss, they usually left the country with little hope that the trickster would be caught, and still less that any of the cash they had parted with would be recovered. By the time the police got to hear of the matter the trickster had invariably gone abroad, there to lie low until his victim had left for home, the date of his departure having been ascertained during their brief "friendship." Then in the 1930s there came a change. It was decided that the victims of such frauds should be invited to return to England, all expenses paid, and give evidence against those who had swindled them. From then onwards, following the prosecution and conviction of several well-known confidence tricksters, this type of crime diminished rapidly. Meanwhile, other forms of fraud, such as mock auctions, bogus charities, and so on, continued to flourish until new legislation made it easier to secure convictions in these sorts of cases as well.

Perhaps people are less gullible nowadays than they used to be. Perhaps all the publicity that is given to crime in the press and on TV, coupled with a greater awareness of the value of money, brought home by the bleakness of the economic climate, has made the public less easy to hoodwink. Whatever the explanation, I am sure the sort of story on which the confidence trickster used to rely would find very few takers today. Most con men, for some reason or other, were either Irish or Australian, with a gift of the gab and a charm of manner that would have enticed a duck off a pond. They worked in pairs, and time and money would often be freely spent in setting up arrangements for a coup. A favorite story was that of a fabulous treasure hidden in Spain. The way of working the trick was relatively simple. A wealthy visitor—always one traveling alone—would find himself in conversation in the bar of his hotel with another lone traveler like himself. Let us call them X and A, respectively. At A's suggestion they would embark on a sight-seeing tour and in the evenings go to theatres, night clubs, and so on. During this time A would find out all he could about X's financial status, how credulous he might be, and his immediate plans. If he were satisfied of X's potential as a victim, the next move would be for them "accidentally" to bump into a "stranger," B, professing to be another traveler on his own like themselves. A would suggest that if X were agreeable B should be asked to join them on their various excursions. After two or three days B would begin to speak mysteriously of a fabulous treasure hidden somewhere in Spain. Pressed for further details, he would reveal the story, often producing newspaper cuttings (specially printed) to confirm it. He would explain that he had not got enough capital to exploit the situation and would suggest that if he and X were to finance the operation jointly the treasure could be secured for them both. It is a tribute to the rogues who engaged in this type of fraud that by their powers of persuasion and convincing personalities they managed again and again to deceive hard-headed and experienced men of business. Yet the final episode in the plot was usually so childish that it is difficult to believe that anyone of sound mind could have been taken in by it. A would begin to express some doubts about the story. B would react by protesting at this lack of confidence in him. As proof of his integrity he would be prepared to put £5,000 in cash into an attaché case and let A or X disappear with it for half an hour. This being agreed to by A, B would later meet them both with a locked case supposedly containing his £5,000. He would now stipulate that they should show the same confidence in him by each in turn trusting him with the same amount, to be taken away and brought back in the space of half an hour. So first of all X would take B's case out for a walk, then B would take A's, and finally it would be X's turn to entrust his case to B. After B's departure, A would ask X to mind his case for a moment while he went to the lavatory. And that would be the last that X would ever see of either of them. When he opened A's case he would find it filled with paper.

Such a story may be difficult to credit. Nevertheless, for many years during the summer months the con men were used to reaping a rich harvest. In one case a wealthy Australian sheep farmer went all the way back to Australia to collect more than £10,000, which by an agreement made while he was in London, he then took to Cairo and handed over to his new-found "friends." Eventually the friends were traced, arrested, and convicted and most of the money recovered.

One of the most successful figures in this shadowy world,

whose ingenuity and daring raised him head and shoulders above the rest, worked entirely on his own. He was known as Michael Corrigan, alias Cassidy. His real name was never established, nor his birthplace, but it was believed that he was Irish. I first came in contact with him while I was in Brussels, where incidentally I also met for the first time another of his kind, a Pole named Solomon Wälkau, alias Rechland, then a petty crook living on his wits, who was later to become known in England as Sydney Stanley, and whose activities, revealed by the Lynskey tribunal in 1949, were of considerable embarrassment to the British government.

Corrigan, at the time I came across him, was living in style, owned race horses, and entertained lavishly. One evening in a bar he became very aggressive towards some Englishmen and threatened to get them kicked out of the country, intimating that he had some sort of pull with the authorities. I happened to hear of this, so I made some inquiries, as a result of which I got in touch with Scotland Yard to find out if anything were known about him. The reply that I received was that Corrigan was not only known but wanted. In London he had told someone a tale about his having taken part in a Mexican revolution, whose triumphant leader, out of gratitude for his support, had granted him large oil concessions. Corrigan had produced impressive documents (which, of course, were bogus) on the strength of which he had secured several thousand pounds from various people with which to develop his nonexistent concessions. Subsequently he had been charged with fraud, but had absconded while he was on bail. All this I passed on to the Belgian police.

The use of a false name is punishable in Belgium by imprisonment. Corrigan was arrested and being unable to prove that Corrigan and not Cassidy was his real name, he was convicted, and on his release from prison was deported. Being British, he was put on a cross-channel boat and at Dover was met by Scotland Yard officers. Later he was tried and found guilty of fraud in connection with his alleged adventures in Mexico and, having a number of previous convictions, was sentenced to five years' imprisonment.

After his release he was soon to be seen about in the West End and at race meetings. He apparently had no difficulty in getting money out of the people he mixed with, in spite of his reputation, which was well known. Indeed, it was such that no one cared to prosecute him for fear of being made to look a fool. As one man who had parted with £1,000 said to me, "Everyone knows Corrigan, and if prosecuted I should be the laughing stock of my friends."

Corrigan's most spectacular and possibly most ingenious coup was brought off during the period of the Spanish Civil War, at which time the Japanese were invading China. Destruction, though on a smaller scale, was also taking place at Tottenham in north London, where an old church was being pulled down. It is difficult to imagine that anyone could have seen any significance in the simultaneous happening of these three events, but Corrigan with characteristic ingenuity devised a connection.

Soon after the work of demolition had begun at Tottenham, he appeared on the scene, talking with an American accent, and expressed his sorrow at what was happening to the old church, where, so he said, he had attended Sunday school as a child. When he was twelve his parents had emigrated to the United States, taking him with them, and there his father had amassed a fortune. That fortune he had now inherited and thus being enabled to retire, he had come over for the first time since leaving England to revisit the scenes of his childhood and early religious teaching, only to be met by this sorrowful sight. The impression he made was of a man much afflicted, likewise of one not only philanthropic, but also deeply devoted to his religion; for after asking many questions, he announced that he would have the entire church, after it was dismantled, sent to his home town in the United States and re-erected there. Negotiations followed and it was arranged that every stone should be marked, packed, and delivered to a warehouse in London until arrangement could be made for this shipment to America.

Act Two took place in the Spanish Embassy, where shortly afterwards Corrigan presented himself and produced documents purporting to be from the War Office, giving him an option for the purchase of guns and munitions awaiting disposal at Woolwich Arsenal. The Spanish government, being in need of arms, and having no reason to disbelieve Corrigan's circumstantial story, supported as it was by documentary evidence, agreed to pay some £20,000 as soon as the goods were put on board for shipment to Spain.

The scene of Act Three was the Chinese Embassy—a similar story was told, similar documents produced, and a similar agreement signed.

By the time these transactions were completed, the demolition of the church was finished and its stones packed and stored in a London warehouse.

Corrigan then presented bills of lading to the two embassies, showing that the armaments he had promised them had been loaded on board and were to be discharged at Marseilles for transshipment to their respective countries. He then received payments accordingly.

At Marseilles, however, when the "goods" were being unloaded, one of the cases crashed on to the quay and broke open, disclosing the contents, which consisted not of armaments but of marked building stones and rubble. The other cases, on being opened, were all found to contain similar material.

Inquiries were started and eventually Corrigan was arrested and charged with forgery and false pretences. However, at his trial, the jury found him guilty on one count only, that of false pretences, for which he was sentenced to two years' imprisonment.

At the end of the war, he was hauled in by the Fraud Squad on yet another charge. After appealing in court he was refused bail and remanded to Brixton Prison. No doubt he realized that with his long record he would be bound to get a heavy sentence if he were convicted. For one accustomed as he had been to living a gay and extravagant life, such a prospect must have seemed pretty grim. At any rate, it was one that he found he could not face and he hanged himself in his cell.

The motive of the con man is the same as that of almost all

criminals—easy money. But his mentality is rather different. To perform a confidence trick, or indeed to cheat someone by a carefully thought-out ruse, requires more than mere ingenuity; it requires an ability to put on an act and maintain it, sometimes at considerable risk of discovery, for days or even weeks on end. It requires a knowledge of the ways of the world, especially the fashionable world, and an acute appreciation of the vanity, snobbishness, cupidity, and other traits of character that make a man or woman an easy victim for the con man.

One of this breed, who was no less plausible or ingenious than Corrigan, but whose frauds were on a more modest scale, was Frank James White, generally known in his various encounters with the police as Eustace Hamilton Hargreaves, and also on occasions as Mortimer Colefax, Vincent H. Gunnell, Ian Spencer Hayward, and Nicholas Revenell. These aristocratic-sounding aliases disguised White's humble origins. Born at Hammersmith, of working-class parents, he went to an LCC elementary school, which he left at the age of fourteen, and after spending a year as an office boy, helped his father, selling flowers from a street barrow. He was first convicted at the age of twenty-one and thereafter was in and out of prison until he died. By 1933, when he was twenty-eight, he already had eight convictions for stealing by trickery, most of his offenses being thoroughly despicable in that they traded on the simplicity of people who, unlike Corrigan's victims, could ill afford to lose anything, let alone hard-earned savings. Though most of his crimes took the form of elaborate hoaxes, he was not above petty theft. On one occasion having arranged with a secretarial agency to supply him with a typist and a typewriter, he called for her in a car, then on the pretext that he needed some carbon paper, sent her into a shop to buy some. As soon as she had gone, he drove off with the typewriter. Another time he offered a lift to a woman carrying a heavy suitcase. During their journey he asked her to look and see if he had got a flat tire. When she got out of the car he drove off.

On the occasion of his conviction in 1933, he was sentenced to five years' imprisonment. He told me afterwards that during

this time he worked in the prison library and studied assidu-
ously. He was naturally intelligent and very plausible and had
developed a good personality and an attractive manner. With
these attributes he was able, without arousing suspicion, to
stay at expensive hotels and mingle with people of standing
while posing as a rich landowner.

In planning his coups Hargreaves (the name by which I
knew him best) deliberately set out to exploit those interests
or innocent ambitions that sustain the inner lives of most of
us. Probably the most successful of his swindles was one concerned with what he called the Royal College of Literature
(strange as it may seem, there is nothing illegal in using the
prefix "royal" to give an air of respectability to any dubious
enterprise). The scheme was addressed, through newspaper
advertisements, to people who wanted to make money by
writing. All they had to do was to apply for membership in the
College, granted on payment of two guineas, then send in their
work for it to be criticized and for advice to be given on how to
improve their style, and so forth. An astonishing number of
people, running into several thousands, fell for this simple
trick. More astonishing still was the fact that the police received not one complaint about the matter. This meant, of
course, that we were powerless to proceed against Hargreaves, except for a technical offense under the Business
Names Act. But in view of his record our suspicions were
naturally aroused.

Other fanciful schemes which he launched, also with a view
to ensnaring those with literary interests, were the Books
Censorship Board, the Faculty of Criticism, the Public Relations Council, the Library Users' Association, and the Durham
University Press. As their titles suggested, the purposes of these
concerns were the improvement of literature, better service
from public library, and so on. Whatever their object, the same
participation fee of two guineas was all that was asked for.
Once it had been paid there was nothing more for the aspiring
author to do. Nor did he receive any further word from Mr.
Hargreaves, another of whose schemes was the Immunity
Trust. Householders were invited to rent, for the sum of 3s 6d

a quarter, a small plate to be fixed to their front doors, and if the house was entered by thieves the Trust would offer a large reward for the tracing of them. If the reward was not claimed within three months, the householder himself could claim it. The odd thing was that none of these schemes, except for the Royal College of Literature, seemed to have had much success, which was perhaps the reason that Hargreaves persisted in trying to think of new ideas.

He next came to the notice of the police in 1938 at the time of the Munich crisis when he started to advertise a scheme called ARP Crisis Evacuations. Applicants were sent an official-looking form giving details of accommodation available in "safe-areas" in the event of war. Such accommodation could be reserved by applying to the "Area Controller of Reservations," with of course the usual two-guinea registration fee. Owing to the intervention of the police, however, the scheme never got off the ground. As a result of his frauds Hargreaves spent most of the war in prison.

On several occasions thereafter he was charged with various types of fraud and twice convicted. In 1952 he was again convicted, this time in connection with a bogus scheme concerning a cider company. From an address in the Cotswolds he advertised the scheme in reputable newspapers and in the glossy magazines and netted altogether some £11,000 from the sale of shares. Charged with converting this money to his own use, he was remanded on bail of £500, though this was strenuously opposed by the police. It was indicative of the confidence he was able to inspire that he found a guarantor in a gentleman he had recently got to know in Gloucester, where he was living at that time in his usual impressive style.

What followed was equally indicative of Hargreaves' brazen ingenuity. He jumped his bail and though he had had to surrender his passport, he next turned up in Paris, where we heard that he had been sentenced to imprisonment for using a false name and passport, which were in fact those of one of his gardeners. On his release he was issued a certificate, by the British consul in Paris, with which to travel to England. Unfortunately, by the time this information reached the Yard he

had disappeared again. Later it transpired that he had somehow got to Marseilles, where he had gone to the port and had
found out when the next ship from England would be arriving,
and where its next port of call would be. He was told the name
of the ship, the times of its arrival and departure and that it
would be bound for Tangier. He then went to an English bookshop and there got into conversation with a girl working for
an English firm with an office in Marseilles. From her he learned
the names of various English businessmen living in the city.

The ship he had been told about duly arrived and after he
had watched it leave he went hastily to the British Consul to
whom he spun a tale of woe. Giving his name as Wilfred John
Wadley, he said that he had come ashore to look round Marseilles, had lost his bearings, and returned to the quay just in
time to see the ship sailing away, and with it all his luggage
and his passport. He had urgent business to do in Tangier and
asked if the consul would issue him an emergency passport.
Several of the English business community would vouch for
him, he said, and quoted the names he had been told in the
bookshop. Having had considerable experience of his astonishing glibness and convincing manner, I can very well understand that his story was accepted without question and a
passport, valid for one week only, was issued to him. What I
have never understood was how so sharp a rogue could have
been so foolish as to do what Hargreaves did next. He wrote to
a newspaper in London offering to sell his life story—his
exploits, as can be imagined, were not unknown to the press
and public—for payment in dollars, it being his intention to
make his way to the United States. In this he underestimated
the cooperation between the Moroccan police and Scotland
Yard and as a result was arrested and imprisoned for using a
false name and a false passport. On his release from prison he
was deported to Gibraltar where Scotland Yard officers met
him with a warrant for his re-arrest. On the charge relating to
the cider company he received a sentence of eight years' imprisonment. It was his twelfth conviction, and he died while
serving it.

Hargreaves' character offers a classic example of that conflicting combination of intelligence and stupidity that characterizes so many habitual criminals. He had been charged more than thirty times with various offenses, most of which had resulted in his being imprisoned or fined. Too lazy to follow a steady occupation, he had nevertheless spent endless time and ingenuity in devising plans for making easy money, yet being well aware of the risks he ran in doing so.

The Alibi That Failed
(10)

☞ I never considered a senior detective to be fully blooded until he had investigated a difficult case of murder. In all, I was concerned in some fifty murder cases in which about two-thirds of the murderers were found guilty, the rest being found guilty of manslaughter. Of those convicted of murder only six were hanged.

I cannot help feeling that on the whole, the abolition of capital punishment has been a mistake. Its main result appears to be that the number of murders has increased. Admittedly the increase is not large, but that there should have been any increase at all is to my mind sufficient proof of the deterrent effect of the death penalty, and to have cast away so powerful a weapon in the armory of crime prevention imposes an unfair burden on both the public and the police.

Since my days in the police force a generation of young criminals has come into being who have little regard for life.

They know that if they are caught and convicted of murder in connection with a robbery their spell of imprisonment may well be no longer than they might have got for the robbery itself.

In the twenties various gangs were active in London and if one of their number stepped out of line he was liable to be disciplined by being beaten up or slashed with a razor. I saw quite a few of these gentry in hospital after they had been dealt with, but none of them would ever talk. I am convinced that what stopped their pals from liquidating them, as was happening at this time among the gangs in America, was the certainty of going to the gallows if they were caught and sentenced.

The fact that only six of the several dozen murderers with whom I was concerned were hanged indicates how carefully the Home Secretary considered every murderer's case, giving due allowance to the circumstances of the crime, to the emotional element, such as jealousy, rage, or despair, and to the mental history not only of the murderer, but of his or her family back to the grandparents' generation. Such cases are very different from that of the criminal who deliberately arms himself with a gun; his only purpose must be to use it if anyone should try to stop him from committing his crime. For thugs of this type I have no sympathy whatever.

In dealing with a case of murder, the detective in charge, after the preliminary procedures have been gone through, has then to consider whether the killing was unpremeditated or planned, and what was the motive for it. Most unpremeditated murders are committed out of jealousy, revenge, or a sense of grievance and are therefore not difficult to solve because motive and opportunity can usually be ascribed to a particular person. Sexual murders of women and children are often the most difficult to deal with because as a rule they are committed by opportunists to whom one victim is as good as another, so that there is nothing about the circumstances of the crime that can readily be associated with any particular individual or group of individuals.

Planned murders are on the whole infrequent. They usually

fall into the following categories: political assassination by shooting or planting bombs; the elimination of a troublesome or awkward spouse (the cases of Crippen and of Bywaters and Mrs. Thompson come to mind); killing in order to obtain money or property, as in the cases of Frederick Seddon, the poisoner, and George Haigh, who disposed of his victims in an acid bath.

Occasionally you get a case like that of John Christie, the Kensington murderer, who killed in order to gratify his necrophilic urge, but such cases are rare.

When one views the matter dispassionately, murders that are deliberately planned are much the most fascinating to deal with. To unravel the strands of a calculated and ingeniously woven plot is usually much more interesting psychologically and forensically than locating a thug who has stabbed someone in a street brawl or shot a bank clerk. There have been cases in which murderers have based their crimes on something they have read or seen in a film or on TV. I have often wondered whether John Merrett, better known as Ronald Chesney, who murdered his wife at Ealing in February 1954, got the idea of his crime from a novel or a film. It certainly had all the ingredients of a who-done-it—a wife who was an encumbrance; the temptation of an inheritance dependent on her death; and a beautiful German blonde who was the murderer's mistress. Although I was not personally in charge of the investigation, its progress at every stage was discussed with me at Scotland Yard by Detective Superintendent Daws, who handled the inquiry.

Chesney was born at the wrong time. He should have been a seventeenth-century buccaneer roaming the Caribbean Seas. In appearance he was large and robust and wore a black beard and a gold earring in one ear. His life from start to finish was one of lawlessness and violence. At the age of eighteen he was tried in Scotland for murdering his mother by shooting her, but a verdict was returned of Not Proven, that conveniently evasive formula that absolves the Scottish juryman's conscience and leaves a permanent taint on the person acquitted. Chesney was charged in the same connection with forging checks in his mother's name, and for this was sentenced to a term of imprisonment. After his release he turned up in the south of England where he stayed with a former friend of his mother's, a Mrs. Menzies, whose daughter Isabel he later married. The marriage soon broke up, and his wife returned to her mother. Before long Chesney was in trouble once more, being convicted of fraud, and was again sent to prison.

At the age of twenty-one he inherited some £50,000 from his grandfather, of which £10,000 was left in the form of a trust fund for the benefit of himself and his wife, the money becoming available to either of them in the event of the other's death. Chesney very soon spent the rest of the money and thereafter until the outbreak of war in 1939 he lived by petty crime. He then joined the Royal Navy and eventually became a lieutenant commander. After the war the economic conditions in Europe gave him scope for exercising his talents as a smuggler and black marketeer.

In the 1950s his wife, then aged forty-three, with the help of her mother, an old lady of seventy-three, was running a home for old people at Montpelier Road, Ealing. Assisted only by a girl of eighteen, Eileen Thorp, they looked after nineteen elderly people, three of whom were bedridden.

Chesney at this period was living in Cologne. From time to time he came over to England and saw his wife. His presence thus became known to her two chows, who were by no means friendly to strangers. In the light of what happened later, Chesney's familiarity with the dogs was a factor of considerable importance.

At seven-thirty on the morning of February 11, 1954, Eileen Thorp took a cup of tea up to Mrs. Chesney, but found that she was not in her room.

She then took some tea to Mrs. Menzies, whose room was on the ground floor, but she was not there either. The beds in both rooms, however, appeared to have been slept in. After looking for the two women without finding them, she took the residents their breakfast and discovered to her surprise that no one had seen either Mrs. Chesney or her mother. As the front door was still bolted on the inside, as it always was at night, she became alarmed and sent for the police.

The officer who took charge of the case was Detective Superintendent Daws. During some twenty years which he had spent with the Flying Squad, Daws had acquired a formidable reputation in the criminal world for the care and persistence with which he carried out his inquiries, and he tackled the Chesney case with his usual thoroughness. His first step on arriving at Montpelier Road was to have a look at Mrs. Chesney's bedroom. He then went to the bathroom and there found her lying dead in the bath. Mrs. Menzies' room was then searched and her body was found hidden behind a sofa.

Although the plug was in the bath, when Mrs. Chesney's body was found in it, the bath was empty. She was wearing a nightdress and a pink woolen jacket and her hair was wet and soapy. Except for two small bruises on each of her arms there were no marks of violence. Mrs. Menzies, however, had evidently made a fight for her life and there were wounds on her head and her hands. A stocking was tied tightly round her neck.

Both the bedrooms had obviously been tidied up, though on Mrs. Chesney's sheets there were found to be some small smears of blood and others were discovered on the floor and wall in Mrs. Menzies' room. Here also a dented metal coffeepot was found with bloodstains on it; evidently it had been used as a weapon with which to batter the old lady on the head.

As the front door had been locked and bolted, Daws' next move was to try and find out how the murderer had got into the house. He found that on the French windows leading to the garden there was a faulty catch and that they could be opened from the outside without much trouble. What interested Daws no less was the fact that as soon as the two chows saw him they started barking and tried to bite him. This, Miss Thorp said, always happened with strangers. She had not heard them at all during the night; from which Daws concluded that whoever had entered the house, it must have been someone whom the dogs knew.

Examination of the house for fingerprints showed that the bath had been carefully wiped all round, removing any prints that might have been there. This examination was, of course, part of the routine procedure in a case of murder, as was the taking of blood samples, hairs from the victims' heads, and clippings from their nails.

During the inquiries that followed, a number of facts came to light. Most significant of these was the fact that Chesney stood to benefit by £10,000 through his wife's death. Also that he had repeatedly asked her to divorce him, and that he was at present living in Cologne and associating with a German girl. It also emerged that Mrs. Chesney, in whose room a lot of empty bottles were found, was a very heavy drinker.

The case had, of course, been given wide publicity in the press and shortly after inquiries had started a solicitor informed Daws that Chesney had written to him and asked him to tell the police that he had not been to England since 1953, but was ready to come over to prove that he had no connection with the murders. Up to that moment there had been no hint from the police that they associated him in any way with the crime.

Meanwhile, Daws' inquiries were bringing to light quite a number of interesting facts, and various people also began to come forward with information. Among other things Daws found that Chesney had been sent to prison in 1951 for fraud and that while he was there he had met a man called Boyd to whom he had explained that a trust fund had been set up by which either he or his wife would benefit, according to which of them died first. He had said to Boyd that he would pay £1,000 to anyone who would murder Mrs. Chesney. He had also told the same story to another prisoner, called Pickersgill.

Chesney was the first of the three to be released and when Boyd came out, Chesney met him again and renewed his suggestion about the murder of his wife. His idea was that Boyd should run her down with a car, but Boyd said he would have nothing to do with such a plan.

After Pickersgill was released Chesney approached him and offered him £2,000 to shoot Mrs. Chesney—£20 down and the rest as soon as the job was done, payable in France where

Pickersgill was to go and meet Chesney. But Pickersgill, too, declined to have anything to do with the matter.

Eventually, Chesney met a third man whom he had known in prison and put the same proposition to him, but with the same result.

A fourth man, an ex-RAF officer whom Chesney got to know, was also asked to dispose of Mrs. Chesney and was actually given a postdated check for £1,000, payable as soon as Chesney had come into his inheritance from the trust fund.

In view of all this information inquiries were made to find out whether Chesney had returned to England immediately before his wife's death, but there was no evidence of his having passed through any of the ports. Nevertheless, extensive house-to-house inquiries resulted in the discovery of two or three people who on the evening of February 10 had seen a man answering to Chesney's description hanging about in the vicinity of his wife's house, but obviously not wanting to be seen. It was also discovered that Chesney had arrived in England at the end of January and stayed till February 4, a week before the murders took place, when he left for Holland by boat from Harwich. His conduct at the time of his leaving was rather odd. First, he bumped into a policewoman to whom he apologized for knocking her down; and when he was going through the customs he joked about being a smuggler. It would seem that the customs official had not got much sense of humor; taking Chesney at his word, he had him searched and, of course, took his name. It seemed pretty obvious that all this was done by Chesney for the purpose of drawing attention to his presence, so that those concerned would be able to vouch for his having left the country a week before the murders took place.

Daws continued with his inquiries to try and find out whether Chesney could have returned to England secretly, and discovered from Special Branch officers who had been on duty at London Airport, that on February 10 a man answering Chesney's description had arrived from Amsterdam with a passport in the name of C——, and had left London Airport at 8 A.M. the next day to return to Holland.

C—— was eventually traced and interrogated. He denied having a passport and said he had not left the country since 1945. However, he eventually admitted that he had met Chesney in 1953, and that Chesney had then told him that he had obtained a passport in C——'s name, but of course had used his own photograph. C—— said that he was angry about this, but Chesney had given him £10 to keep his mouth shut about what he had told him and promised him some more money later on.

After discussing these developments with Daws, I decided to send him and another officer over to Germany to interview Chesney. But they got there too late; before they arrived Chesney shot himself. Daws' departure for Germany had been publicized in the press and Chesney had obviously realized that the net was closing.

Chesney's suicide did not end Daws' task. The end of a murder case does not come automatically with the arrest or death of a suspect. It still remained for Daws to establish beyond doubt that Chesney had murdered his wife and his mother-in-law and to this end it was essential to prove how and when Chesney had come to London.

Daws' inquiries proved conclusively that on February 8 he had left Cologne with his German girlfriend and that they had gone to stay at a hotel in Amsterdam. The girl, whom Daws saw afterwards, confirmed this and said that they had stayed in Amsterdam until the morning of February 11. When Daws reported this to me on the telephone, I told him to send the officer who was with him to Amsterdam to check the German girl's story. The officer went there and found the story was correct, except for one important omission, which was that Chesney had quitted the hotel on February 10, leaving the girl alone that night, and had rejoined her on the afternoon of the eleventh, when they had left to return to Cologne.

Chesney's photograph was shown to a number of people— and with his fine physique and black beard he was easy to remember—at Amsterdam airport; on the plane in which he had traveled to London (in the name of C——); at London airport; and on the plane by which he returned to Amsterdam. All of them identified the photograph as that of Chesney.

Daws examined Chesney's body and saw that the hands and arms were bruised and scratched. He telephoned to me about this and said that the authorities refused to let him bring the body over to England. I asked him to get their permission for the arms to be amputated so that he could bring them back for examination and this they agreed to. Accordingly Daws brought back with him not only Chesney's arms, but also his clothes and a sample of his hair, all of which were sent to the laboratory for examination.

The results were very interesting.

Mrs. Chesney's pink woolen jacket and a slipper which Mrs. Menzies had been wearing were both found to have some hairs on them which were similar to Chesney's. On the right leg of Chesney's trousers were some bloodstains belonging to Group O, the group to which Mrs. Menzies' blood belonged, but not Chesney's. Stains of the same sort were found on his cardigan, on which there were also some dog's hairs similar to those of Mrs. Chesney's chows; there were also hairs similar to Mrs. Menzies', and some blue and red fibers similar to the material of her head scarf. Significance was added to the presence of these fibers by the pathologist's report which indicated that they had probably been stained with blood *before* they adhered to Chesney's cardigan. Finally, scrapings from underneath Chesney's fingernails were found to contain minute but still identifiable fibers of bright pink wool similar to that of Mrs. Chesney's woolen jacket.

From all of this evidence it was possible to reconstruct the events that had taken place. On February 10, Chesney, using the name C——, had traveled from Amsterdam, had managed to enter the house through the French windows without alarming the two chows who, of course, knew him, had found Mrs. Chesney drunk, forced her into the bathroom, and there drowned her, afterwards soaping her hair to make it look as though, under the influence of drink, she had died accidentally while washing her hair. Then, as he was leaving, he had run into Mrs. Menzies, who could of course have identified him, so he had no alternative but to kill her too. After a terrible struggle he had finished her off with the nearest thing to hand, the metal coffeepot. If he had managed to kill Mrs. Chesney only, her death might well have been recorded as an accident.

In any case, he hoped he would have been able to prove that he was in Holland at the time. This was his big mistake. His carefully concocted Amsterdam alibi collapsed as soon as it was investigated.

Before he committed suicide Chesney had written to a solicitor in England telling him that he intended to do so and asking the solicitor to see that the £10,000 payable under the trust fund in the event of his death should go to his German girlfriend. However, as the jury at the inquest of his wife and his mother-in-law returned a verdict of murder against him, the object being to cheat the administrators of the fund, his request was ignored.

This case, as I have said, had all the features of a carefully planned fictional murder in which the motive would have been the basis for a good plot. But Chesney had overlooked one thing: the search for a motive would inevitably lead the police in time to fix their suspicions on him. Given the patience, long experience, and painstaking attention to detail of a detective like Daws, coupled with the cooperation of scientists and foreign police forces, it might be said that Chesney, in spite of all his careful preparations, never had a chance.

Coronation
Day
(11)

☞ And now, as a change from crime, something very different. As Deputy Commander of No. 1 District, which covered the western and southwestern areas of London, to which I was appointed in 1952, I inherited a "manor" that included Buckingham Palace, Whitehall, and the area around the Houses of Parliament and Westminster Abbey. Maintaining law and order in this region may not sound as tough a job as trying to do so in Brixton or Soho, but being an area in which most of the important ceremonial events of the year take place, the officer in charge of No. 1 District is continually involved in making arrangements for these events and ensuring that they pass off smoothly.

Few people watching the Guards trooping the color in the presence of the Queen, when there are usually about 2,000 police on duty, or the state procession of some visiting royalty to or from Buckingham Palace, can have any conception of the immense amount of preparation that is involved to make sure that everything goes without a hitch. Naturally, the spectator, cheering the Queen as she rides past on horseback, escorted by the Household Cavalry in their shining helmets and cuirasses (some of which, incidentally, were actually worn at the battle of Waterloo and still bear the marks of musket balls)—the spectator does not stop to think of all that has gone into the planning of the ceremony. But without such planning, and without the meticulous rehearsals and stop-watch timing, it would be all too easy for these spectacular events to end in chaos.

Soon after the Queen's accession in 1952 a Coronation Commission, under the chairmanship of Prince Philip, was appointed to initiate and supervise arrangements for the occasion. As soon as the date had been agreed upon—and many people at home and overseas had first of all to be consulted—a decision had to be made about the route the procession was to take to and from Westminster Abbey. The distance from there to Buckingham Palace is comparatively short, less than two miles. But in order that as many people as possible should be able to see the Queen, the return journey to the Palace via Hyde Park, Oxford Street, and other main thoroughfares, covered about ten miles.

The plan was for the Queen to travel in state from the Palace, her procession being preceded at intervals by seven other processions that included members of the royal family, rulers and representatives from abroad, and Commonwealth prime ministers. In addition, there was to be a carriage procession from St. James's Palace to the Abbey, consisting of members of the diplomatic corps and other distinguished visitors. For the return journey these various processions were to be joined by naval and military contingents, with their bands, from Commonwealth countries, and other groups representing various civilian organizations and public services. It was estimated that the total length of the procession would be more than two miles.

All this having been decided, it became the responsibility of the police to work out potential plans for ensuring not only the safe and smooth progress of this immense cavalcade, and for controlling the vast crowds that were to be expected, but also to ensure that the 8,000 guests invited to the ceremony in the Abbey could get there unimpeded and at the right time. (For the majority this meant being in their seats by about 7:30 A.M.) All in all, it was one of the most gigantic problems of organization that Scotland Yard has ever had to tackle, with some 40,000 police on duty, very many drawn from forces outside London.

Arrangements also had to be made to accommodate the large number of troops and civilian units that were to take part in the procession, and to "feed and water" the whole of this multitude, for which purpose encampments were set up in the London parks.

Our first job was to start checking up on all known political extremists (not only those at home, but, through Interpol and foreign police forces, those abroad) who might be likely to try and cause incidents, whether by shouting slogans or scattering leaflets or by some other and more sinister means. Political assassination is fortunately a very rare occurrence in Britain, but with so many important foreigners coming to London as guests of the Queen, the possibility, if remote, was not one to be altogether dismissed, and it was the duty of the Special Branch to keep a careful and prolonged watch on anyone who it was thought might be a potential troublemaker.

Meanwhile, there were plenty of other, less clandestine jobs to do. Every structure or balcony along the route on which people might climb or congregate had to be examined to make sure they were safe and would not collapse. Manhole covers in the road and trap doors and pavement lights had to be examined too, and the inspection and testing of all these possible danger points over a densely built-up route of some ten miles was a very long job.

We had also to consider where to erect crush barriers, and meetings were held with government departments and private contractors to arrange for the siting and safety of the very large number of stands, both public and private, that were to be put up for spectators all along the route. Many streets were to be blocked off by hoardings or used to accommodate troops and vehicles standing by while the ceremony in the Abbey was going on, and very careful planning was called for to ensure that essential services would not be interfered with. This meant evolving or coordinating plans with various public bodies, water, gas, electricity, and transport authorities, the GPO, and the ambulance and fire services, so that in an emergency they would be able to get to the spot where they were needed.

Another matter that had to be carefully considered was the provision of first-aid posts, extra public lavatories, and centers for the collection and care of lost children. It was anticipated that the crowds along the route would number at least five million and that all these facilities would be in considerable demand. In the event, apart from minor accidents and illness, three women in advanced states of pregnancy had to be taken to hospital, one baby being born en route, and two people collapsed and died. Of the children who got lost, I believe all were eventually restored to their rightful owners.

One thing that we had failed to anticipate disclosed itself only a short while before the procession to the Abbey was due to start. In making a final survey of the route, I noticed to my consternation that at all the women's lavatories that had been installed—but not at the men's—there were huge queues. It had not occurred to anyone concerned with the arrangements that a lady visiting a lavatory invariably spends a few moments in nose powdering or some other act of titivation. At 9:30, little more than an hour before the Queen was due to arrive at the Abbey, there was a queue at one lavatory of more than three hundred women. A quick decision was needed and I switched a sign from a near-by "Gents" to transform it into a "Ladies."

As soon as we knew the route that had been chosen we had to start making parking arrangements for the thousands of cars that would be bringing visitors to London. We also had to work out plans for parking the cars and carriages of the 8,000 guests going to the Abbey. This meant making a survey of squares and streets for miles on either side of the route and estimating the number of extra cars that could be parked in these areas. Anyone wishing to come to London on the day of the coronation had to apply for a permit, stating at the same time where they intended to go to watch the procession. They were then issued with a windshield label showing where their car was to be parked. All this took an immense amount of plotting and planning, the value of which was shown by the comparative ease with which the many thousands of cars were parked and afterwards retrieved by their drivers.

Those who had been invited to the Abbey received detailed instructions, worked out at the Yard, as to what time they were to leave their houses or wherever they were staying, by which route they were to travel, the time at which they were to arrive, and the route of their return journey. In addition to special labels and passes, each of them was issued with a 260-page booklet giving all these details for everyone concerned.

It had been laid down by the Coronation Commission that there were to be no cars in the procession. This posed a difficult problem. A few noble families were able to muster historic coaches, but not many people had carriages in working order and the whole country was scoured for horse-drawn vehicles still suitable for use. They were not easy to find. Most of them eventually came from seaside towns where in the summer months they plied for hire along the front. A more decrepit lot of vehicles I never saw. All of them had to be tested and most of them considerably refurbished to put them in proper shape, and even then some of them still looked in imminent danger of collapse. From the Abbey door where I was stationed, I thought that they might still do so. One of our biggest headaches was to find a carriage for the late Queen Salote of Tonga, a lady of ample proportions. I had a few anxious moments as I watched her re-entering her landau after the ceremony was over, but she covered the route in triumph and without a hitch.

In order to avoid confusion and reduce the possibility of mishaps it was decided to have two rehearsals of the various processions. The arrangements provided for the eight that were to come from Buckingham Palace, and the longer one from St. James's Palace, to reach the Abbey at various times between

8:30 and 10:30 A.M. (For the other 8,000 guests the deadline for arrival was eight o'clock. In fact, to their credit the last of them arrived at ten minutes past eight.)

The first rehearsal showed the wisdom of foreseeing its necessity. It ended in complete chaos. It began at 4 A.M. on a Sunday morning, so as to interfere as little as possible with traffic, and in the hopeful expectation that at such an early hour there would be few spectators. But the press had given a lot of publicity to the fact that rehearsals were to be held and many thousands turned up to watch, adding the complication of crowd control to that of the timing and maneuvering of the long trains of carriages and the masses of troops. Except for the coachmen and horses from the Royal Mews, very few of those taking part had had any experience of this kind of thing, with the result that carriages overshot their carefully prepared stations, or found that they had not sufficient room to back or turn, or else they lagged behind, or got involved with other sections of the procession. Though, as I say, only two rehearsals had been scheduled, it was decided that a third was necessary and on the day all went well.

In contrast with these tremendous and elaborate preparations, one of the most vital operations of the whole affair was conducted with a complete absence of fuss or publicity. A day or two before the coronation. Mr. Mann, the Crown Jeweler, accompanied only by a police officer in plain clothes, collected the crown, orb, and scepter, and the rest of the royal regalia, the value of which is beyond computation, from the Jewel House in the Tower of London and took it in a car to his place of business, where he cleaned everything, and then took it to the Abbey, again without any sort of guard or escort except for the Chief Superintendent, as before. After the ceremony was over, this priceless collection was returned to the Tower in the same way, transported with as little fuss as if it were luggage being taken in a taxi. One can imagine the publicity and the spectacular cavalcade of armored vehicles with a motorcycle escort that would have seemed indispensable to accomplishing such a journey in New York or Chicago.

The coronation was on a Tuesday, but on the previous

Sunday crowds began to gather all along the route. By Monday they were camping out on the pavements, with bivouacs rigged up for children to sleep in and meals being cooked on alcohol-burning stoves. Later in the day it began to drizzle, but nothing seemed to dampen the enthusiasm of the crowd. At 4 A.M. on Tuesday I made a tour of my part of the route and in spite of what must have been a decidedly uncomfortable night—and for some, two nights—everyone appeared as cheerful and good humored as most London crowds are when out to enjoy themselves.

At 6 A.M. I placed the various police contingents in position and soon afterwards the troops began to arrive, followed at about seven o'clock by the first Abbey guests. Then came members of both Houses of Parliament and foreign visitors, and eventually the Speaker of the House of Commons in a coach drawn by four horses whose normal duty was that of pulling brewers' drays. The coach had no brakes and being very heavy, it overshot the Abbey door and had to come full circle in order to deposit the Speaker correctly.

Finally, in the state coach drawn by the famous Windsor Greys and escorted by the Household Cavalry, the Queen arrived with Prince Philip. As she stepped from the coach Big Ben began to strike eleven. Hearing the first stroke, I was glad to think we had had those three rehearsals.

It was about two o'clock before the Queen emerged from the Abbey, wearing her crown, and re-entered the state coach for the ceremonial drive. Long before Her Majesty appeared, the foremost contingents of the procession had assembled far away along the route, and soon after the Queen's coach had set off, the first of the 8,000 guests began to emerge, some going to Old Palace Yard near the Abbey and others to Westminster School, for luncheon. By 4:30 they had all left and the neighborhood of the Abbey and Whitehall was clear of cars. Their place was taken by an army of scavengers and dustmen who began to clear up the tons of paper and the many thousands of cartons and bottles and all the other refuse which the crowd had left scattered about for miles along the route.

I cannot say I was sorry that it was nearly over. For two

nights I had had almost no sleep. A very considerable burden of responsibility had now been lifted from my shoulders, and the long months of planning and preparation had at last come to an end. It was, I must admit, with a feeling of relief that I went across to my office at the Yard and had a cup of tea.

But there was more to come. For two or three days immediately after the coronation, the Queen and Prince Philip made their way through various parts of London and wherever they went there were enormous and enthusiastic crowds. In the evenings, too, the same sort of demonstrations took place in front of Buckingham Palace. All this involved long hours of duty for the police, who had already been at full stretch for several days, but nowhere was there any breakdown in the arrangements. I felt we had good reason to be proud of all the men and women on whom had rested the responsibility for making sure that everything went well.

Operation Digit

(12)

In spite of there being a permanent and widespread interest in crime—you only have to look at TV, read a newspaper, or go into a bookshop to realize how true this is—the majority of people have only the haziest idea of what it is that the police actually *do* when they have to investigate a major crime. That is to say, how they set about making their inquiries, the planning and staff work that is necessary, the briefing of detectives, the consultations with experts and other authorities, how the evidence is collected and what is done with it, how clues are interpreted, and so on. And certainly no member of the public whom I have ever come across has any conception of the enormous number of separate inquiries that is usually involved, nor of the sort of scientific assistance that is often required.

An account in detail of the investigation into the killing of June Devaney at Blackburn in 1948 may be of interest because it provides a classic example of the interdependence of the human and technical elements in criminal investigation, and shows how success was achieved by the combined deductive and scientific processes on which the solution of a complicated case will often be found to depend. (It will be realized that the following account refers to conditions as they were in 1948 and that changes may since have occurred in respect of various matters to which reference is made.)

In the early hours of May 15, 1948, the body of June Ann Devaney, aged three years and eleven months, was found in the grounds of Queen's Park Hospital, Blackburn, where she had been a patient in the children's ward. She was an only child, the daughter of a laborer, and had been admitted to the hospital two weeks before suffering from pneumonia. She was well-developed for her age and in bed she might have been mistaken for a child of six or seven. She was due to have been discharged on the morning on which her body was discovered.

Blackburn is a town of 110,000 inhabitants and is the center of the Lancashire cotton-weaving industry. There are some 35,000 houses in the town, most of them working-class dwellings. Queen's Park Hospital consists of a number of buildings with a total frontage of about a quarter of a mile, standing in grounds of more than 70 acres. There is a high stone wall all round the grounds, except in the northwest corner where there is a disused quarry some 60 feet deep. At this point soil erosion had caused the wall to collapse and as a temporary measure a fence made of chestnut paling had been put up.

Entrance to the hospital is by the porter's lodge, where the identity of everyone who goes in or out is recorded, as are the names and addresses of patients' visitors.

At the time of the murder there was in the hospital a number of mental patients, aged and infirm persons, maternity cases, operative cases, and children, each of these categories occupying separate wards. In addition, there was a casual ward where tramps were accommodated for the night, their average number being about ten. The total population of the hospital, including the staff, amounted to some 1,200 persons.

The children's ward was a small one situated on the ground floor at the end of the hospital farthest from the porter's lodge. In the ward were twelve cots and on this particular night, May 14, 1948, June Devaney was the eldest of the six patients.

At 12:20 A.M. on May 15 the night nurse in charge of the children's ward, on her way to the kitchen to start getting their breakfasts ready, saw June asleep in her cot. About twenty minutes later she heard a child's voice and went back to the ward, but found nothing wrong and returned to the kitchen.

At 1:20 A.M. she went into the ward again and noticed that the door of a porch leading to the grounds was open, but thought nothing of it as the door had a faulty catch and often opened of its own accord. She then noticed that June was missing from her cot. The drop-side of the cot was still raised, suggesting that the child must have been lifted out. (The cot was specially designed to prevent children from getting out and the top rail was about four feet from the level of the floor.) Beside the cot was a glass vessel known as a Winchester bottle, containing sterile water, which the nurse had seen about an hour before standing on a trolley at the end of the ward some six yards away from the cot. The nurse noticed some footprints on the polished floor near the cot which she thought had been made by someone with bare feet.

The nurse raised the alarm and the staff of the hospital began to search the grounds, but found no trace of June.

At 1:55 A.M. the police were notified and as soon as they arrived a more systematic search of the grounds was carried out. As a result of this, at 3:17 A.M. June's body was found lying near the boundary wall of the hospital some 283 feet from her ward. The Chief Constable, the Detective Superintendent, and the police surgeon were notified and arrived on the scene at 4 A.M.

The body had been found lying face downwards in the grass with the child's nightdress partially lifted and dirty, as though she had been rolled about on the ground. It was obvious that she had been brutally raped; blood and fluid were exuding from her nose and vagina and her left buttock had been severely bitten. Death appeared to have been caused by her body having been swung violently against the stone wall.

The hospital was immediately sealed off and Scotland Yard was asked to send assistance.

A special squad of officers began at once to make inquiries into the movements of every member of the staff and every patient at the time of the murder.

A bloodhound was brought to the hospital and after being given a scent from the child's bed and the footmarks on the floor of the ward, it cast about and eventually followed a trail leading directly to the child's body. There the scent ended.

A search by the police showed a trail in the grass which led to where the boundary wall joined the chestnut fence. Here there was a small gap in the fence, and on the other side of this gap a narrow ledge skirting the edge of the quarry. By careful maneuvering along this ledge it was possible to reach a lower road which led to the town.

In conjunction with Scotland Yard officers, a biologist attached to the Yard's Forensic Laboratory made a thorough search of the area of the crime and took numerous samples from the scene, among them some bloodstained grass; some hairs adhering to another patch of bloodstained grass; hair and fibers from the wall near which the body was found; hairs adhering to a bloodstained stone in the wall; a portion of the stone itself, also bloodstained; hair from another bloodstained area of the wall; and a grass leaf bearing stains. From the window of a room adjoining the ward fibers were taken, and more fibers from footmarks on the floor of the ward.

After photographs had been taken and the police surgeon had made a cursory examination of the child's body, it was removed to the police mortuary.

Fingerprint experts examining the floor of the ward were able to show that someone had entered through the porch door, walking in stockinged feet, and had crossed the ward to the trolley where the Winchester bottle had been standing. The footmarks went along the wall, and there were indications that someone had visited each of three cots in turn and had stopped at June's, where the bottle had been placed on the floor. The toes of the prints near the cot were at right angles to it and actually under its edge.

The footmarks were 10¼ inches long and though they were only fragmentary—the pressure of the feet having made micro-shallow indentations in the thin layer of polish—by getting down to within a few inches of the floor they could be seen by specular reflection; that is, from the way the light fell upon the marks.

Several kinds of powder were applied to the floor for the purpose of making the prints more easily visible, but none had any effect, so the prints were circled with white chalk in order that they could be located from a standing position.

Eight of the most complete and distinct right and left foot-prints were photographed, also by specular reflection, and then labeled. (Orthochromatic and processed plates were used in a half-plate camera. Lighting was by one 500-watt bulb.)

In order to take the photographs it was necessary to tilt the camera at an angle. It was appreciated that this would cause considerable distortion to show on the negative; so along each print was placed a 15-inch ruler, which was included in the negative, and when the negative was later placed in the en-larger, it was possible, by using the ruler as a standard, to make the necessary adjustments and reproduce the footprints in ac-tual size and true perspective.

A very close examination of the footprints showed that they had been made by stockinged feet, one print showing quite clearly the texture of the fabric of the sock. An examination of wax scraped off the floor where one of the prints had been made revealed certain fibers embedded in it which were not visible to the naked eye.

It was obvious that the person who had walked in stockinged feet across the ward had picked up the Winchester bottle from the trolley. A careful examination of this bottle showed at least twenty palm- and fingerprints. It was noticed by the fingerprint experts that some of these had been made quite recently and that the fresh prints were much larger than the old ones.

After the latent impressions on the bottle had been photo-graphed and developed, it was put into a place of safety and a thorough examination of the interior of the ward was started. In particular, anything that could bear latent fingerprints was taken for examination.

After a search lasting fifteen hours, and examination of the hospital staff, the following points were established:

1. no member of the staff had been in the ward in their stockinged feet;
2. the Winchester bottle was normally kept on the trolley at the north end of the ward, and not on the floor beside June's cot;
3. none of the staff had carried the bottle from the trolley and put it on the floor.

The fingerprint experts now took finger and palm impressions of everyone who had had legitimate access to the bottle and of various other persons who had any right or reason to go into the ward. This involved the subsequent comparison of over 2,000 prints with those found on the bottle in order to eliminate from the inquiry the staff of the hospital and those who had legitimate access to it. A simplified scheme was introduced for the purpose of identification, which required the taking of only the left forefinger impression and the left thumb impression of each person who had to be interviewed.

Eventually it was established that with the exception of ten palm and fingerprints on the bottle, all the other fingerprints found outside and inside the ward had been made by persons with legitimate access to the premises. It was significant that the only impressions on the bottle which were not identifiable were those which had been freshly made.

The impressions on the bottle consisted of a left thumb print, left fore-, middle, and ring fingerprints, and a left palm print. There were also impressions that appeared to have been made by the right middle and ring fingers. The remaining three were fragmentary finger and palm impressions. Of these impressions, three had been made by a simultaneous grip—these were the left fore-, middle, and ring fingerprints. A left thumb print appeared on another part of the bottle and it was reasonable to assume from its size and texture that it was the impression of a digit of the same hand, which had made the three impressions simultaneously.

A postmortem examination revealed that the child's death was due to shock caused by a fractured skull and extensive injuries to the vagina and internal organs which were consistent with rape. It was also found that the bite on the child's buttock had been made before death, as had a bruise on each of the groins.

Various specimens were taken from the child's body by the biologist from the Forensic Laboratory. These specimens (listed below), together with the child's nightdress, the specimens already collected, and the fingerprints on the Winchester bottle, were all clues and were to be of special significance after the murderer had been arrested. They included, besides the fibers which had already been taken:

1. fibers from the window of the room adjoining the ward;
2. fibers found on the child's body;
3. a single pubic hair found in the area of the child's genitals;
4. hair from the child's head;
5. blood from the child's heart;
6. a vaginal swab;
7. a rectal swab.

On May 18, after extensive inquiries, the police discovered that shortly before midnight on May 14, a taxi driver had picked up a man in the center of the town on the road which leads to the hospital, and had driven him to Queen's Road near the quarry on the outskirts of the hosptial grounds. There the man had got out of the taxi and was last seen by the driver going towards the quarry. The driver had not noticed anything special about the man's appearance, which he was only able to describe in general terms, but said that he had spoken with a local accent.

By this time the investigating officer had formed the following conclusions:

1. all males in the hospital and all persons having legitimate access to the ward having been eliminated from the inquiry by fingerprinting, the footprints found in the ward and the fingerprints on the Winchester bottle were undoubtedly those of the murderer.
2. the wanted man was a local resident with knowledge of the hospital and its environs, this being apparent from the fact that only a person with such knowledge could negotiate the edge of the quarry in the dark.
3. the man must be reasonably tall. A small man could not have taken the child out of the cot without lowering the drop-side; nor would such a man be likely to have feet 10¼ inches long.
4. the murderer's clothing would be bloodstained.

Having arrived at these conclusions, how best to use the murderer's fingerprints for the purpose of identification was the next question.

In spite of the immense scale of the operation it was eventually decided to take the fingerprints of every male in Blackburn of sixteen years old or more, who were known to have been in the town on May 14 and 15. The Mayor of Blackburn was approached and through the press an appeal was made to the public for their cooperation, it being emphasized that when the prints had served their purpose, they would be publicly destroyed. The Mayor himself volunteered to be the first person to have his fingerprints taken.

Public feeling about the murder was extremely strong and it was found that with very few exceptions the male population of the town was willing to cooperate.

A special squad of twenty local officers, who were taken off all other duties, was appointed to the task of taking the left thumb and forefinger impressions of all those who came into the prescribed category. To ensure that the fingerprint check would be systematic, it was carried out to a prearranged plan. The electoral register was used to ensure that every one of the 35,000 houses in Blackburn was visited. These registers are prepared each year on June 30 and record the names of everyone over the age of 21 who is entitled to vote. Blackburn is divided into fourteen voting divisions, which are subdivided into three, four, or five sections according to the size of the area. For further convenience these subsections are arranged in alphabetical order by streets or roads.

Equipped with fingerprint cards and ink pads, the twenty officers were sent out every day to cover preselected districts street by street. Inevitably, a considerable number of return visits had to be made where the men or youths to be fingerprinted were unavailable.

While all this was being done inquiries were being made about persons not residents of the town, but who were in Blackburn on the night in question. Every night the results of these inquiries, together with the completed fingerprint cards, were handed to the officers in charge of the squad.

The information concerning people who had been in Blackburn on the night of the crime resulted in inquiries being made not only in all parts of the United Kingdom, but in almost every country in Europe, as well as in Australia, Canada, Egypt, India, Singapore, South Africa, and the United States. In all these places persons were located by the police and fingerprinted in order to eliminate them, if possible, from the inquiries.

An index was kept by four women police officers to deal with the daily flow of fingerprint cards, which were sent from Blackburn to the fingerprint headquarters and after comparison with the register these were returned to Blackburn, stamped CANCELED.

In view of the nature of the crime male persons in the following categories were also interviewed and fingerprinted:

1. about 4,000 who had been discharged from mental institutions in the north of England, many of them being of low mentality and some of whom had been convicted for various forms of indecency;
2. about 3,000 of foreign nationality, including some German prisoners of war and Polish army personnel living in camps within a radius of twenty miles of Blackburn. This precaution was suggested be-

cause of the biting of the child's buttock, biting
being unusual in Britain, but occurring frequently
on the Continent in crimes of indecency;

3. persons with epilepsy or schizophrenia, who might
possibly have committed the crime during a temporary blackout;

4. persons known to be suffering from venereal disease. These were included because of a mistaken
but accepted notion among certain people that
venereal disease may be cured by sexual intercourse with a virgin or a young child;

5. persons suspected of committing sexual offenses
contrary to nature (*e.g.* homosexuals);

6. persons known to have attempted suicide;

7. tramps and others included in the itinerant population of the area, who might be familiar with the
hospital;

8. all persons missing from home in the United Kingdom at the relevant period.

After a lapse of two months the murderer had still not been
found. This seemed to suggest that in spite of the careful and
methodical process of checking that had been adopted there
must still be a number of people whose fingerprints had been
missed. It was therefore decided that an attempt should be
made to trace these persons through the local Registration
Officer. Ration books were still in use at this time and in Blackburn new ration books were issued to the public between June
30 and July 18. But before the issue of a book, a form included in the book for the previous year, giving the applicant's
name, address, date of birth, and National Registration number, had to be completed and returned to the Registration
Officer. Only after this had been done was a new book issued.
These application forms were afterwards filed in alphabetical
order at the Registration Office.

On July 18 fingerprinting was suspended for two weeks and
the squad that had been engaged on this task moved to the
Registration Office. A system was evolved whereby details on
the list of fingerprints that had so far been taken were compared with those on the ration books. From the resulting par-

ticulars it was eventually possible to compile a list of people who had been missed out during the first check and house-to-house fingerprinting was resumed on August 9.

On August 11, one of the fingerprint squad obtained the prints of Peter Griffiths, an ex-Guardsman, aged twenty-two, living at 31 Birley Street, Blackburn. His card, with others, was sent for checking to the fingerprint headquarters the same day. On August 12, after a thorough examination, it was established that Griffiths' fingerprints were identical with those found on the Winchester bottle.

Griffiths' name had not appeared on the Electoral Register because at the time of its latest revision (*i.e.*, June 30, 1948) he had been too young to qualify as a voter.

On Friday night, August 13, almost thirteen weeks after the murder, Griffiths was arrested by Scotland Yard officers. When told he was going to be arrested for the murder, and after being warned that anything he might say would be taken down in writing and might later be given in evidence, he replied, "What's it to do with me? I've never been near the place."

On the way to the police station he turned to the officer in charge of the case and said, "Is it my fingerprints why you came to me?" He was again cautioned and the officer said, "Yes." When Griffiths arrived at the police station he said suddenly. "Well, if they are my fingerprints on the bottle, I will tell you all about it."

Shortly after this, at Police Headquarters, he made a lengthy statement admitting his guilt. That same night he was charged with June Devaney's murder. After being charged, he was told that he was not obliged to have his fingerprints taken unless he wished, as they might be used in evidence. However, his answer was, "All right, you can take them."

His fingerprints and palm prints, after comparison, were found to be identical with ten of the twenty fingerprints found on the Winchester bottle.

Later the same day certain articles of clothing were taken from Griffiths' home and the suit which he had worn on the night of the murder was recovered from a pawnbroker's shop. These were sent at once to the Forensic Science Laboratory.

The suit, on microscope and chemical examination, was found to be marked with human bloodstains which appeared on the lining of both side trouser pockets and inside the trousers at the bottom of the fly. This blood, classified as Group A, was of the same group as the sample taken from the child's heart.

Bloodstains were also found in the following positions on the jacket:

1. on the lining at the bottom of each sleeve;
2. on both lapels;
3. on the right front above the top button and inside the right edge in the same region;
4. on the top button and near the right shoulder;
5. inside the right bottom front.

Tests at the Forensic Science Laboratory revealed the following facts:

1. fibers removed from the window were identified as being the same as fibers found on the accused's suit;
2. fibers taken from the child's body were found to be woolen fibers ranging in color between blue and violet, agreeing exactly with those of the accused's suit;
3. the hair removed from the region of the child's genitals was identified as being that of an adult. (As the accused refused to give a sample of his pubic hair, a comparison could not be made.)
4. on the child's nightdress were found a number of woolen fibers similar to those taken from the accused's suit.
5. blue and red woolen fibers from the footprints found in the ward matched those of a sock removed from Griffith's home.

Griffiths was 5 feet 10½ inches in height. He was a local man with a good knowledge of the hospital grounds and had in fact been a patient in the block from which he took June Devaney.

His clothing was bloodstained, and he was identified by the

taxi driver, previously interviewed, as the passenger whom he had dropped near the quarry.

In a signed statement Griffiths confirmed that after committing the murder he had left the grounds by the same route as that by which he entered them (*i.e.,* round the top of the quarry).

Griffiths appeared at Blackburn Borough Magistrates' Court and was eventually committed for trial at Lancaster Assizes on October 15, 1948. On that date he pleaded "Not Guilty" and the whole of the evidence for the Crown was presented. The fact that such a mass of detailed and circumstantial information was available was a tribute not only to the conscientiousness of all those who had taken part in the inquiry, but to the vital importance of ensuring scientific investigation of every clue that was susceptible to such examination and to the precise, thorough, and extensive inquiries made by the police.

The defense attempted to show that Griffiths was a schizophrenic and was insane when he committed the crime. This evidence was rebutted by the Medical Officer from Liverpool Prison, who had had Griffiths under continual observation since his admission to the prison on August 14 and had reached the conclusion that he was sane when he committed the crime.

After an absence of twenty-three minutes, the jury returned a verdict of guilty and Griffiths was sentenced to death. He was hanged at Liverpool Prison at 9 A.M. on November 19, 1948.

On November 3, in the presence of the Mayor of Blackburn, journalists, and press photographers, the 46,500 fingerprint cards relating to those who had been eliminated from the inquiry were pulped at a local paper mill.

The successful conclusion of this inquiry demonstrates four basic rules of criminal investigation:

1. the importance of police officers ensuring that material found at the scene of a crime is not inter-

fered with in any way. In this case careless handling of the Winchester bottle, the most vital clue of all, would have made it—and consequently other clues—useless;

2. the necessity for the immediate summoning of experts to deal with data found at the scene of a crime.

3. In a case in which public feeling is aroused, advantage should be taken of the situation to seek the public's assistance and cooperation. It was realized in this case that much useless information would inevitably be submitted, but among that which would be received there could be something of vital importance. In this particular case it was the statement made by the taxi driver.

4. The value of close cooperation between police forces both at home and abroad. In this case the cooperation of forces overseas as well as in Britain was given freely and rapidly.

The solution of the Blackburn murder was based on a thorough understanding of the value of prompt and efficient police procedures and the fullest utilization of scientific techniques. The decision to undertake fingerprinting on such an extensive scale—no such operation had ever been attempted before and involved the taking of more than five times as many prints as had been taken in the Potter's Bar murder case—reinforced the theory that fingerprinting is the soundest medium of identification.

The Great Train Robbery
(13)

☞ At 6:15 P.M. on August 7, 1963, the Royal Mail Train left Glasgow for its nightly journey to London. On the way it stopped at various stations where additional coaches were put on and more mail, both registered and ordinary, was picked up. The last stop was at Rugby, where the amount of registered mail taken on brought the total which the train was carrying to over £2½ million. This was well above the sum usually carried, owing to the inclusion of money that had been paid into local banks during the August bank holiday and which was being sent to the banks' head offices in London.

The train left Rugby at 2:17 A.M. for a nonstop run to Euston, but at Sears Crossing in Buckinghamshire it came to a halt, the signal being red. Almost immediately the driver's cab was boarded and he himself attacked by a gang of masked men who stole all the registered mail and then disappeared.

When the train left Glasgow it consisted of a diesel engine, attached to which was a baggage van, then came the coach with the registered mail in it, known as the high-value-packet (HVP) coach, in which men were sorting the mail and putting it into bags. After this came ten more coaches, some carrying bags of mail already sorted, others being used as sorting offices. Altogether there were seventy-seven post-office men on board. Through the train a corridor ran from the rear coach to the second coach, but between this one and the HVP coach there was no communication, nor was there any communication between the HVP coach and the diesel engine.

At Sears Crossing, some forty miles from Rugby, the distant signal being amber and the home signal at red, the driver stopped the train. The time was 3:03 A.M. As both the driver, Jack Mills, and the fireman, David Whitby, could see, the distant signal on the next section was green, so they concluded that the line ahead was clear, but that their signal must be at fault. Whitby got down and from a telephone beside the line, tried to contact the signal box, but could get no reply. He then noticed that the telephone wires had been cut, and at that moment he saw a man standing between the HVP and second coaches. Thinking at first that the man was a postal sorter from the train, Whitby went up and asked him what was wrong. The man started making for the embankment and told him to follow, which Whitby did, assuming now that the man was a railway worker. When they got to the top of the embankment, Whitby was suddenly seized and pushed to the bottom, where there were two more men. One of them clapped his hand over Whitby's mouth and threatened to kill him if he shouted. These two then disappeared, leaving the first man standing guard over Whitby with a cosh.

At this moment Mills, the driver, saw the two men coming from the embankment, and assuming them to be linesmen dealing with the signal failure, he turned to adjust his controls, anticipating that he would be given the all-clear to proceed. He looked around, expecting to see Whitby, but instead he saw a man with a cosh climbing on to the footplate. Mills grabbed the man and tried to force him off, but was struck on the head from behind and fell down, half stunned. In a moment the cab was full of masked men. Mills was told to get up, was again threatened with a cosh, and then pushed into the engine-room. There he saw Whitby, guarded by another masked man with a cosh.

Two or three minutes later, Mills, who by this time was streaming with blood, was shoved into his driving seat and told to start the train. After driving it about half a mile, he was told to stop. At this point, a spot known as Bridego Bridge, a wide piece of white material had been placed across the track, obviously as a marker. Mills was now taken back to the engine room and handcuffed to Whitby. Together they were pushed off the train onto the track and made to lie down on the far embankment with their faces to the ground. Whitby managed to see, however, that only the luggage van and the HVP coach were still coupled to the engine and that the train had stopped on a bridge over a roadway. Parked near the bridge was a large lorry. Mills saw about ten men unloading mail bags from the HVP coach and passing them down the embankment.

A few minutes later, he and Whitby, still handcuffed together, were taken to the rear of the HVP coach and told to climb aboard. By this time, Mills was suffering pretty badly from his injuries and found it difficult to get in. When he did so, he saw the GPO men lying face downwards, and he and Whitby were told to do the same and not to move for half an hour; if they did, they would be hurt.

Later, the post-office men working on the train had their own story to tell. In the HVP coach there was an assistant GPO inspector with four postmen. When the train stopped, they were busy sorting mail and noticed nothing unusual until the train began to move again; then they heard steam escaping from the rear of the coach. They assumed at once that the coupling between their coach and the rest of the train had broken, so one of them pulled the communication cord. After traveling a little way, the train stopped, then suddenly a window was smashed and they realized it was a raid. Immediately they barricaded the doors of the coach with mail bags, whereupon someone outside shouted, "They're barricading the doors—get the guns" (no evidence was forthcoming later that any of the robbers had carried a gun), then a second window was smashed and two men climbed in, both armed with coshes. Others similarly armed, and one carrying an axe, also forced their way into the coach and in less than a minute after the train had stopped it was all over. The five GPO men were herded together at the end of the coach and told to lie down and keep their eyes shut. They heard the mail bags being removed, and then Mills and Whitby were pushed up into the coach. Following the orders they had been given, they all lay quiet for half an hour, then the inspector and one of the sorters got out and started back along the track. On the way, they met the guard, coming forward to see what was going on, and told him what had occurred.

Meanwhile, the other GPO men on the train knew nothing of what had happened. One of them, in the second coach, looking out of the window after the train had stopped, saw a man standing between his own and the HVP coach, then this man was joined by another and both of them moved off towards the engine. The GPO man, assuming them to be railway men dealing with some defect, started going towards the HVP coach and, as he did so, he saw it move forward, then it was hidden in a cloud of steam from the vacuum pipe. When this cleared, he saw that the HVP coach had parted from the rear end of the train and was moving forwards and someone was closing the connecting door; but he still did not realize anything was wrong, though he was puzzled because the signal was red.

When the train stopped at Sears Crossing, the guard was in his compartment in the last coach. Two minutes after it had stopped he heard the brakes go on and saw the pressure gauge go down to zero, so he went along the train to find out what was happening. When, to his surprise, he found the HVP coach had disappeared, he got down to the track and after walking a way met the GPO inspector. The guard went back quickly to his own compartment and put on the hand brakes, then got some detonators and placed them on the track behind the train. He then went back to his compartment to telephone to the signal box, but finding that the wires had been cut, he got out and started walking towards the next station at Cheddington. On the way, having come to the missing part of the train, he hailed another which was passing and which took him on to Cheddington signal box, where he sent for help. The time was 4:15 A.M.

As soon as the guard reported the holdup the local police were alerted and as more information began to come in it was sent to all police cars and surrounding country forces. In the meantime, a fireman from a train on the slow line drove the diesel engine with its two coaches to Cheddington station, and Mills, still handcuffed to Whitby, was taken by ambulance to hospital at Aylesbury, where he had seventeen stitches put into the wound on his head.

One can imagine the consternation that news of the robbery caused at Cheddington station at that early hour in the morning. At 4:30 A.M. local patrol cars and an ambulance went there, and were followed soon afterwards by senior police officers.

Whenever a major crime is committed, there is usually a good deal of confusion among those involved, and it often takes a little while for the police to get a coherent account of what has happened. In this case there were many things to be seen to, as well as inquiries to be made on the spot. All four telephone wires to the signal box had been cut. The green light of the home signal was covered by a man's glove, and the red light, which was still showing, had been connected by wires to dry batteries with a switch and when this was thrown to the "off" position, no lights showed on the signal. The bulb of the distant signal's green light had been removed and wires attached to the amber light, on which there was an "on-and-off" switch; but the batteries had been taken away—in other words, the same method had been used for operating the cautionary amber signal as for the red light on the home signal.

Before the signaling system could be repaired, arrangements had to be made for photographers and fingerprint experts to deal with the diesel engine and the HVP coach; the scene of the holdup had to be carefully examined for clues, and Whitby, the guard, and the occupants of the HVP coach had to be questioned. All this took time. Mills, the driver, was too badly hurt to be questioned at length, and consequently some hours elapsed before a true picture emerged of what had happened.

About an hour after I got to my office on the morning of the robbery an early edition of the evening paper was brought in, giving a brief account of what had happened and putting the amount stolen at nearly £1,000,000. (We were to learn later, incidentally, that the numbers of only 1,579 of the stolen notes had been recorded.) Shortly afterwards there arrived a copy of a message that had been circulated to all police forces in England by the Chief Constable of Buckinghamshire, Brig. John Cheney, giving an outline of the story. I tried at once to telephone to his headquarters, but every line was jammed and I could not get through. I had no doubt that the Buckinghamshire police would soon be asking for our help, so I sent at once for the senior officers of the Flying Squad, the London and provincial Crime Squad, and the Intelligence Squad; but with such scanty information as we had got at that time, there was not much to discuss.

Officers in these three squads, all of which are based at Scotland Yard, are hand-picked for their knowledge of criminals of all classes, for what they know about their habits, associates, private lives, and ostensible occupations. Altogether there are more than a hundred of these officers. They work closely together, exchange data, and have their own sources of information, yet not one of them had heard so much as a whisper of any plan to rob the mail train.

Just as our meeting ended I had a telephone call from Brigadier Cheney. He gave me an account of what had happened and asked for the Yard's immediate help. To start with, there was to be a top-level conference at the GPO in London that afternoon.

The news of the robbery could not have come at a worse time. As luck would have it, the Assistant Commissioner of the CID, Mr. (now Sir) Richard Jackson, was at an Interpol conference in Finland, and with him was one of my two deputies; my second deputy was gravely ill in hospital, and five of the six detective superintendents of the Murder Squad were on assignments in the provinces. To increase our difficulties, three other senior detective superintendents from divisions had been sent out of London after urgent requests for help elsewhere, and several other officers were away on holiday. But it was certainly not a holiday month for crime in London: robberies, wage snatches, burglaries, and breakings were on the up and up and every CID officer in the metropolis was working at full stretch.

A considerable number of people attended the conference at the GPO, including members of its Investigation Branch and of the British Transport Police. Detective Superintendent Fewtrell, head of the Buckinghamshire CID, gave an account of what had taken place, but despite the fullest possible search by him and his officers, nothing had been found to indicate who the robbers might be or where they had come from. Only one small point of possible importance was mentioned: Whitby, the fireman, thought that one of the men who had attacked him had a cockney accent.

I had no doubt that the men involved were London criminals. The most sensational and best-planned robberies almost always take place in London or the home counties. Indeed, London has the doubtful privilege of being the place where the cream of the criminal profession live. These gentry are always up to date with the latest police methods and procedures and in this case I naturally assumed that they would know exactly what the police would do as soon as the crime was discovered. One thing they must have known was that roadblocks would be set up on all roads leading away from the scene of the crime, so that the chances of making a clean get away would not be too good. Criminals who hijack trucks in London often run them into a hide-out not far from where they have stolen them, unload the contents, then drive them somewhere else and abandon them. I felt there was a possibility they might have done the same in this case. Looking at it from their point of view, it seemed likely that if they had made such arrangements, their hide-out would have to be within half to three-quarters of an hour's run from Sears Crossing, so as to enable them to get under cover before the alarm went out. As two or more lorries had probably been used, and as the robbery had taken place at night, the robbers had obviously made their get away through country lanes to a hide-out not more than twenty miles away.

During the conference at the GPO someone asked why there was so much more money on the train than usual. The explanation was this: banks all over the country must, of course, carry enough funds to meet their day-to-day demands, but if a bank anticipates that it may need more than the normal amount of floating cash, the head office is asked to send more. Conversely, if a bank accumulates more money than it is likely to need for its day-to-day business, the surplus is sent to the head office. At certain times during the year, particularly at holiday resorts, large sums in cash are paid into local banks by hotels, restaurants, shops, and so on. Tens of thousands of people spend the four annual bank holidays away from home and most of the money that is spent is in cash. All this money is paid into the bank on the Tuesday after the bank holiday, and when it has been counted and checked, is sorted into bundles of £5,000 and £1,000. This procedure is usually completed by the next day, Wednesday, and the money is then posted as registered mail to the various head offices in London, so that it can be recirculated. Anyone handling this mail—banking, post-office, or railway staff—would have known that on the night of Wednesday, August 7, certain mail trains would be carrying registered packets of far higher value than usual. The leaders of the gang that robbed the train must also have known this well before the holiday and had obviously prepared their plans accordingly.

It was explained at the conference that two mail trains, one from Scotland and one from the west country, travel to London every night. They carry no passengers, only railway and post-office staff. The ordinary mail is sorted in the rear coaches and all the registered mail is in the HVP coach. When the mail reaches London, the bags are delivered to the GPO in Islington and then distributed.

The railway signaling system was also explained to us. Each section of a railway track has two signals, distant and home, both of which are controlled from a signal box. But there is also an automatic device in each section of the track by which the train, as it passes a signal at green, changes these two signals to amber and red (caution and stop) respectively, and until the train has passed out of that section those colors remain unchanged. At each home signal there is a direct line to the signal box, and if a train is delayed by the signal for more than three minutes, it is the fireman's duty to telephone to the signal box and ask the reason for the delay, so as to make sure that the signal is not at fault. Therefore it was obvious that in the gang there must have been someone with a detailed knowledge of signaling mechanisms and procedure, and also men who knew how to deal with the couplings and vacuum pipes between coaches.

Listening to Mr. Fewtrell's account of what had happened, it struck me as strange that there had been no indication in the Sears Crossing signal box that anything unusual had occurred. At 2:58 A.M., the train had passed the box at Leighton Buzzard; at 3 A.M. the man on duty there had received an indication that the distant signal at Sears Crossing was out of order. Assuming that this was due to a signal fault, he waited, expecting a telephone call from the fireman of the train. But he heard nothing. Then at ten minutes past three he got a call from Cheddington signal box asking where the train was. He said that it had entered his section, but that though his indicator showed it had passed Sears Crossing signal, it also showed that that section was still engaged. It looked as though there was some trouble either on the track or on the train, so he asked for a linesman to be sent out and informed Euston station. He also arranged for the driver of a train traveling on the second track to Euston to look out for the GPO train and to let Cheddington know of its position.

Unfortunately, by the time this second train went past, the

robbers had completed their operation and were well away. Immediately after they had overpowered the men in the HVP coach, they began unloading the mail bags and in not much more than half an hour had shifted 120, containing 636 packets and weighing in all about two tons. As soon as the last bag was loaded, they all drove off. The rapid removal of such a weight of mail was a pretty good indication that a large number of men had been involved.

When the conference ended it seemed as though there was literally nothing on which we could get to work. However, I suggested, in view of my theory of a possible hide-out, that there should be a systematic search of all empty houses, farms, buildings, abandoned army and RAF camps and any other places within a thirty-mile radius of Sears Crossing where the robbers might have gone to ground to count their loot before dispersing; also that an appeal be made through the press, radio, and television asking anyone who had seen a group of strangers in any particular place to inform the police.

I was not very hopeful, even if my theory should prove correct, that criminals of the robbers' class would have left anything behind that might incriminate them. As in various other big robberies, though we often knew who had committed them, it was not always possible to produce evidence that would stand up in a court of law. On the other hand, with so many men and such a large amount of money involved, it seemed very likely that sooner or later a substantial amount of the cash would find its way into the hands of wives, relatives, or friends of the robbers, and that this sudden prosperity would cause gossip, which in the end would filter its way back to the police. This would at least give us some indication of who the criminals were. Also, I had no doubt that although the need for tight security would have been uppermost in their minds, one or more of the gang—as invariably happens when a large number of people are concerned in a crime—would probably be less discreet than the rest and eventually start to chatter. I did not say this at the conference, it was merely a hope. I knew that time and patience would be needed for any such possibilities to develop.

It was clear that for the time being there was nothing more to be done in Buckinghamshire, except to press on as quickly as possible with the searching of buildings and property. I had taken with me the GPO conference Superintendent McArthur, an experienced officer, and I now told him to go down to the Aylesbury headquarters of the Buckinghamshire police with a detective sergeant and take charge of the search. I then went back to the Yard and saw Chief Superintendent Millen, who was then in charge of the Flying Squad, to whom I had previously given the job of organizing a special section to deal with the messages and information which were already pouring in from the public and officers out on inquiries. In fact, so great was the flow that we had to bring in officers from other departments to help. Much of this information was quickly classified as useless, but anything that seemed to have some possible value was looked into, and within a few days almost half the CID officers in London were involved. These officers had at the same time their own local crimes to contend with, and the strain on everyone concerned was enormous.

During August nearly 2,000 messages were acted upon by the 80 or so officers of the Flying Squad, who searched more than 220 premises. These searches had some unexpected results. Large quantities of stolen property were recovered, and in one raid three men were found in possession of a considerable number of £5 notes, though none were from the train robbery. The three men were busy printing the notes for themselves. Owing to this upheaval in the criminal world, major crime in London virtually ceased during this period, and I heard that the feeling in criminal circles was that the sooner the train robbers were caught the better, so that ordinary crooks could get back to their normal occupations.

While all these activities were gathering momentum, I was in contact every day with Mr. McArthur at Aylesbury, but the searches that had been carried out had brought no results. By this time, it was estimated that the amount stolen was over £2 million, and, undertsandably, the Home Secretary and the Postmaster General were both pressing for information about what the police were doing. So on August 12, I decided to go down to Aylesbury with Mr. Millen to see what was happening.

When I arrived the next morning, Mr. McArthur explained how the searches were being conducted. They were being carried out by small squads of police visiting farms and empty buildings, in an area surrounding Cheddington, and it was intended to spread out farther as each area was dealt with.

As at Scotland Yard, the Buckinghamshire police had been inundated with information. I asked to see all the messages that had come in, and going carefully through them, we found one from a Mr. John Maris, a herdsman, suggesting that Leatherslade Farm, near Brill, might be the robbers' hide-out. This message had been received at 9 A.M. the day before, but for some reason no action had been taken. Later that same day a message had also come from an estate agent at Bicester in Oxfordshire, who had sold Leatherslade Farm some weeks earlier. (In statements issued about our inquiries we had asked estate agents to report any recent sales of property in the Cheddington area.) Two policemen had been told that morning to visit Leatherslade Farm. I felt some apprehension about what might happen, if indeed it was the gang's hide-out and some of them should still happen to be there. But my fears were groundless—the officers could not find the farm.

About noon the local policeman at Brill reported by telephone that John Maris had contacted him and that together they had gone to the farm, which they found unoccupied; but in a cellar were some empty mail bags and postal and banknote wrappings.

Very soon, a cavalcade of police cars was on its way to the farm. It was an ideal hide-out, weedy and desolate, at the end of a narrow lane about a quarter of a mile from the road, from which the farm, lying below a ridge, was invisible. On one side were three dilapidated sheds, which partly blocked the view of the front; the back and another side were screened by orchards.

The farm was a two-story building with five rooms, a large kitchen with a larder, a bathroom, and a cellar, where the mail bags and the wrappers had been found. The larder's shelves were stacked like a supermarket, and in the kitchen there was every sort of utensil you could need. An inventory of food in the larder included 18 tins of pork luncheon meat; 9 tins of corned beef; 40 tins of baked beans; 18 one-pound packets of butter; 20 tins of peas; 38 tins of soup; 15 tins of condensed milk; 34 tins of fruit salad; 16 two-pound packets of sugar; 7 wrapped loaves of bread; and 19 cans of beer. There were also large supplies of cheese. Oxo, Bovril, ketchup, biscuits, cakes, jam, and coffee, half a sack of potatoes, a barrel of apples, a case of oranges, 40 candles, a gas stove, and 17 rolls of toilet paper.

In the upper rooms there were 11 inflatable rubber mattresses, with blankets and pillows, 6 sleeping bags, 20 jackets, 9 pullovers, several pairs of denim trousers, and 20 towels.

Looking at all this, I felt pretty certain that a woman must have given advice about how the place should be equipped and stocked. Nothing, as far as I could see, had been forgotten and the time that must have been spent in buying such a large supply of stuff and bringing it to the farm was an indication that careful planning had been made for a long stay. The amount that had been left indicated roughly the number of men who had been there as being between ten and eighteen.

Everything in the kitchen was clean and tidy. There were no dirty pots or pans, or piles of unwashed crockery, and after making sure that nothing whatever would be touched, I began a tour of the ground round about the house.

On one side we found the remains of a bonfire with a large number of empty tins lying about, indicating a "residence" at the farm of some duration. Near-by was an open pit, freshly dug and no doubt intended for burying the ashes. In one of the sheds near the house were two Land Rovers and an Austin 3-ton truck.

When I had finished inspecting the place, I gave instructions that the farm should be cordoned off and no one allowed to enter the house. Then I telephoned to Scotland Yard and asked for a fingerprint expert to come down with a team and examine the whole farm from top to bottom.

So far, our total knowledge of the criminals was of their thoroughness, skill, and ingenuity in ambushing and robbing the train, and in their preparation and provisioning of a base. I was not at all confident that much would be found in the way of fingerprints; years of experience had taught me not to accept things at their face value and I did not believe that these criminals would be so careless as to leave any prints.

Up to this moment I could see no point in sending a large team of officers to join Mr. McArthur, as I was now certain that the criminals were from London and it was therefore obvious that our inquiries would be concentrated there.

However, we now had a starting point from which to begin the investigation. But we also needed an operational plan and I decided to form special squads to deal with the various types of inquiry that would have to be made. This involved the redeployment of a larger number of officers from various branches of the Yard. First, Chief Superintendent Butler and Chief Inspector Vibart, two of the ablest and most experienced CID officers, each with an intimate knowledge of all the top-class criminals, were brought in to cooperate with Mr. Millen, who was continuing to handle all incoming information. All the officers of the Flying Squad were concentrating on tracing and arresting anyone whom we had reason to suspect of being concerned in the robbery. I also appointed a team to investigate the purchase of the farm, and officers from the Stolen Car Squad to trace the owners and the history of the three vehicles we had found there. Finally, it was arranged that after the fingerprint men had completed their examination, experts from the Laboratory should take over to see what could be found in the way of scientific evidence.

Anticipating that there would be an accumulation of witnesses' statements and of exhibits, Mr. McArthur was instructed to assemble and collate everything in the way of documents, statements, and so on, from every officer engaged in the case, and from this material to prepare evidence and reports in case of a prosecution. In the event, this proved to be a task far beyond our expectations, and it was complicated by several arrests being made in quick succession, which necessitated long hours of work in preparing evidence for the court. By the time the arrested men were committed for trial at the Buckingham Assizes, the prosecution's documents, bound in several volumes, comprised thousands of pages. Besides the originals, copies of much of this material had to be prepared for the judge and jury, as well as for prosecuting and defense counsels. Indeed, looking back, I think that Mr. McArthur probably had the most tedious and complicated task of any that the officers had to carry out. Evaluating evidence as it was submitted, fitting it in with other evidence already received—or finally rejecting it—and sometimes having to obtain additional statements or reports, was like putting together an enormous jigsaw puzzle.

Mr. Fewtrell became what one might call "the reception officer." Individual suspects arrested in London were taken to Aylesbury and handed over to him to be charged. He also had the responsibility of classifying and storing all the exhibits, as well as the money that was recovered, and the preparation of all the forms required by various authorities as the men were charged.

II

While the experts were still engaged in their investigations at the farm, a break came from quite a different quarter. We had circulated to the press, the BBC, and ITV all the information that we had been able to gather, coupled with a request that if anybody should happen to notice someone with a large sum of money in notes, they should at once inform the police. It was to the credit of an astute and sensible lady living in Bournemouth, who had harkened to this appeal, that evidence of considerable importance was uncovered. Her name was Mrs. Clarke and she was a policeman's widow, a fact that may have been significant in her suspecting something unusual.

On the very day that the farm was discovered, Mrs. Clarke had advertised in a local newspaper that she had a garage to let and had had a visit from a man who said he would like to rent it. He had insisted on giving her three months' rent in advance, although she would have been content with less, and paid the amount, £7 10s. 0d., from a thick wad of notes. His eagerness to clinch the deal and the amount of money he seemed to have about him struck Mrs. Clarke as being a bit suspicious, so after thinking things over she decided to tele-phone the police. However, before they arrived the man re-turned with a friend and they disappeared into the garage. When they left, the police having arrived meanwhile, they were stopped and questioned. The answers they gave left some room for suspicion, so they were taken to the police station, where they were searched. One of them, William Boal, had some £118 on him, and the other man, Roger Cordrey, about £160. Boal also had a receipt for the cash purchase of a car, an Austin A35.

The police were not satisfied with their explanations of how they came to have this money and decided to have a look in the shooting brake, which had been left in Mrs. Clarke's garage. With Boal's key they unlocked the brake and in it found two bags, each stuffed with bank notes, and also a pillowcase full of bank-note wrappers.

Both men were questioned again and as a result, the police went to a flat where Cordrey said he was staying and then to a garage where he said he kept his car. The flat and the car were both searched and again large quantities of bank notes were found. Altogether some £141,000 in notes was discov-ered. Following information given by Cordrey while he was being questioned, a house in London belonging to his sister, Mrs. Pilgrim, was searched by the Flying Squad and £850 in £5 notes was discovered. At Boal's address in London the Squad found another £350, also in £5 notes.

Cordrey and Boal were taken to Aylesbury and charged with being concerned in the robbery, and Mrs. Pilgrim and her husband and Mrs. Boal, with receiving part of the proceeds. It was not a bad beginning, thanks in the first place to Mrs. Clarke, but obviously we still had a long way to go.

During the week that followed the discovery of the farm, fingerprint experts had been going meticulously over every inch of the building. After this operation had got under way, I rang up the officer in charge, Superintendent Ray, to find out how things were going. To my surprise he told me that quite a few finger- and palmprints had been discovered and were being photographed. When his team had finished their investigations, about ten days later, he returned to Scotland Yard and began the immense job of checking all the prints that had been found against prints in the records.

Immediately after he and his team had left the farm, experts from the Forensic Science Laboratory took over and began their examination, which included not only the farm buildings, but also their entire contents.

On the day after Mr. Ray got back, he came to my room with photographs of some fingerprints that had been found on the Cellophane wrapping of a travel kit and on a drum of salt, and a palmprint found on a window sill. All of them corresponded with prints already in our records of a man named Charles Wilson. I therefore gave orders for him to be arrested and charged. After his arrest, a check of his fingerprints and of his right palmprint showed that they were identical with those found at the farm. Nothing connected with the robbery, however, was found at his house.

Meanwhile, information, most of which proved on investigation to be useless, continued to come in from all sorts of places, but every one of these reports, however trivial, had to be thoroughly checked, unless they obviously came from mischief makers or self-seeking cranks, who are invariably the bane of every detective in charge of a case that gets wide publicity. Such inquiries take up a lot of time. In the midst of them, a little less than three weeks after the robbery, I began to receive information from various sources which, when put together, gave a fairly comprehensive picture of the crime and those who had been involved in it.

From what we knew already, it was quite clear that this information was substantially accurate—how the signals were manipulated, what happened after the train was stopped, the robbers' return journey to the farm, the share-out, and then the gang's dispersal. All these things were described to me in considerable detail. But far more important than this were the names and descriptions of several men out of fourteen who were said to have taken part in the raid, and certain information about others involved at various stages of the operation.

The share-out began as soon as the gang reached the farm. The money was in separate packets, each with a wrapper round it showing the amount, so the operation was quick and fairly easy. The whole lot was divided into eighteen shares, each of them totaling about £140,000, and by midday the job was done. Only fourteen men had been concerned in the actual holdup; the remaining four shares were for others who had been concerned in preparations for the robbery or had been bribed to give vital information.

I immediately passed the names and descriptions that had been given to me to Superintendent Ray, who checked the files to see if any of the men were known to the police. One of them was called Ronald Biggs. His fingerprints, which were in the Yard's records, were found to be identical with prints that had been discovered at the farm. He was arrested by Flying Squad officers and taken to Aylesbury and charged.

Three other men had been named to me as James Hussey, Robert Welch, and Thomas Wisbey. After certain inquiries had been made, Hussey and Wisbey, and a little later Welch, were arrested and charged. When their finger- and palmprints were taken, they were found to be identical with prints found at the farm.

Other fingerprints on various articles at the farm were identified as those of five men also known to the police—John Daly, Ronald Edwards, Roy James, Bruce Reynolds, and James White. It was found that all of them had disappeared from their homes with their wives and children. Descriptions of them all were circulated to the press and television authorities and were also sent to Interpol.

Another man whose name had been given to me was Douglas Goody. None of his prints had been found, but he was known to be an associate of some of the men who had been arrested or were wanted. It is of interest to examine the Goody episode more closely, as it emphasizes two important factors relative to the detection of crime. One: the value to the police, as shown by the enterprising Mrs. Clarke at Bournemouth, of extensive publicity being given to the physical appearance of suspects; two: the immense amount of trouble that has to be taken to verify or disprove statements made in connection with a crime.

The first person the police went to see was Goody's mother, with whom he lived, but he, like some of the others, had disappeared. The house was searched, but nothing was found to connect him with the robbery. A few days after the search began, an officer at Scotland Yard received a letter from Goody. This officer had come in contact with him at the time of the London Airport robbery in 1962, Goody having been charged with taking part in it, though he was later acquitted. In the letter Goody said that knowing he was believed to be concerned in the train robbery, he intended to lie low until the gang was caught. It had taken eight months and every penny he possessed to fight the charge against him in 1962 and he didn't intend to go through the same ordeal again.

Inquiries revealed that Goody was on friendly terms with a publican in southeast London from whom, on August 22, he had borrowed a car in which he had driven to a hotel in Leicester. It is perhaps worth pointing out that simple though these facts may sound, their discovery involved the careful and prolonged interrogation of a large number of people and constant contact and exchange of information between the Yard and various county police forces.

Chance now took a curious hand in the affair. A woman who worked at the hotel in Leicester thought Goody resembled one of the men whose photographs had been circulated in connection with the robbery. Now the odd thing is this: Goody's photograph was *not* one of those that had been circulated, but everyone was so acutely conscious of the affair that all over the country people imagined they had spotted one or another of the wanted men. The woman in this case told the hotel manager, who sent for the police.

Goody at first denied his identity, but eventually admitted who he was. Later, questioned by Mr. Vibart about his movements on August 8, he said he was in Northern Ireland at the time, so inquiries were shifted to Belfast. There it was established that he had arrived with his mother and a friend on

August 2, but had left by himself on August 6, two days before the robbery. He was again interviewed, but now said he had nothing more to say. The police, while not satisfied with his story about the length of time he had spent in Ireland, and although they knew that his was one of the names that had been given to me, still had no evidence at that time on which they could detain him.

Knowing the sort of men we would be dealing with, I had given instructions that any officers sent to detain them were to be accompanied by an expert from the Forensic Science Laboratory, who was to make the searches and take charge of anything that looked as though it might have some bearing on the case. The officers were also instructed simply to caution the wanted men before they arrested any of them and not to say anything more, though they should note anything that might be said voluntarily. I wanted no suggestions made at the trial that any officer giving evidence of an admission by one or other of the accused was telling lies, or that anything tangible that might be introduced as scientific evidence could be said to have been planted by the police. Both are familiar allegations by professional criminals and any suspicion that such allegations might be true could have been damaging to the case for the Crown. As it was, not a single challenge on these grounds was made by any of the defending counsel.

The precaution of sending a forensic scientist along with the police on their inquiries turned out to be a useful move. The officer who went to interview the publican with whom Goody had stayed was accompanied by Dr. I. G. Holden. Among various objects of clothing that Dr. Holden took away from the room where Goody had been sleeping was a pair of suéde shoes. When these were examined at the Laboratory some traces of yellow paint were found on the soles. Dr. Holden gave it as his opinion that this paint must have been wet when it came in contact with the shoes.

The Austin truck found at Leatherslade Farm had been painted yellow and in the shed where it had been discovered was a squashed tin of yellow paint, of which there were several large splotches on the ground. Chemical examination of samples of this paint by the forensic experts showed it to be the same as that which had been found on Goody's shoes. On the strength of this discovery he was arrested and charged.

The officers looking into the history of the trucks found at the farm had now completed their inquiries. The new Land Rover, bearing false license plates, we found to have been stolen in the West End eighteen days before the robbery; the other had been bought at a sale in July and sold a month later to a man calling himself Bentley, but who answered to the description of one of the men still wanted, James White. The Austin truck was found to have been bought at an auction also in July, for £300 cash by a man who gave what were subsequently found to be a false name and address.

During these developments Inspector Mesher of the Fraud Squad had been uncovering the history of Leatherslade Farm to establish how the gang had come to occupy it. Briefly, the owner, a Mr. Rixon, who had bought it a year earlier, decided in the early part of 1963 to sell it, and placed it in the hands of three agents. At about the end of May 1963, two men came to look at it. One was Leonard Field, who represented himself as the potential purchaser, and the other was Brian Field (they were not related), who described himself as managing clerk to a solicitor, John Wheater. Eventually £5,500 was agreed as the purchase price and the agent received from Wheater a check on deposit for £550.

The next development was interesting, bearing in mind the date of the train robbery—August 8. Mr. Rixon was informed by his solicitor that although the balance of the purchase price would not be available until August 13, the purchaser was anxious to take possession on July 29. This was finally agreed to on condition that 7 percent interest would be paid on the balance until the date of completion, and on July 29 Mr. Rixon vacated the farm.

After the robbery Leonard Field was not traced until September 9, when he denied knowing anything about Leatherslade Farm. But during this time extensive inquiries brought to light other evidence and on the strength of this both Fields were arrested and charged with conspiracy to rob. Later, it was decided to arrest Wheater and charge him with being concerned with the Fields in conspiring to rob and also to obstruct the course of justice.

In the case of Brian Field there was additional evidence which came to light in an unexpected way. On August 15, a Mr. Ahern was traveling by motorcycle to the factory where he worked at Dorking in Surrey. With him as pillion passenger was a lady who also worked there and to whom he gave a lift every day. As a rule, Mr. Ahern went by car, but at this particular period his car was in for an overhaul. Now, both he and his lady passenger were of mature years and she understandably felt some reluctance about riding on his pillion on a busy main road, so on this occasion they traveled by various side roads. At one point where the road became steep Mr. Ahern's engine got overheated, so he stopped to let it cool down—again that little bit of luck that I have mentioned before. At the spot where they pulled up the road was wooded and Mr. Ahern, to kill time, wandered in among the trees. He had gone a few yards when he saw lying on the ground a pigskin holdall, a plastic bag with a zip top, and a leather traveling case. Thinking they might have been left accidentally by picnickers, he opened the plastic bag to see if there was anything in it to identify the owner. Sure enough there was—but it was certainly not the sort of thing Mr. Ahern expected. The bag was crammed with £1 notes. He went back to the road, stopped a passing car, and asked the driver to call the police, deciding with admirable good sense to disturb nothing and to wait by his find until the police arrived. When they got there they discovered a fourth case. All four cases were taken to Dorking police station, where they were found to be packed with bank notes, amounting to £100,900.

This was not all. Stuffed down a hole in the lining of one of the cases was a bill from a hotel in Bavaria, showing that a Herr and Frau Field had stayed there in February. Inquiries through Interpol showed that the couple were Brian Field and his wife. Before his arrest, Field was shown the bill and admitted it was his, but denied knowledge of the bag in which it was discovered. On the day he was arrested his home was searched, but nothing relating to the robbery was found.

It was never established who dumped these notes, but it seems likely that the money was one of the four shares that I was told were put aside for those who had helped the robbers in various ways.

By now I had a more or less complete picture of the planning and organization of the robbery, which had involved several months of careful research and preparation. It has often been said that a mysterious mastermind was behind the affair, but in fact it was the joint plan of some five or six men. They knew without question that two days after the bank holiday the mail train would be carrying a vast sum of money being sent by local banks to their head offices. They had also obtained information about banking and post-office procedures, as well as about the train itself—the time and place most suitable for its ambush; its route, running schedule, and make-up; how its personnel were distributed throughout its length; the method of detaching its couplings; the signaling system by which its journey was controlled, and innumerable other matters. In particular, a lot of careful thought must have been given to the time and place at which to stop the train. It had to be brought to a halt at a spot suitable for the rapid removal of the mail bags to vehicles waiting near the track, and also close to a point where the signals could be manipulated. In the event, the place chosen was an isolated spot in open country some three-quarters of an hour's run from Rugby.

To have found a spot that fitted these requirements so precisely must have involved a careful survey of miles of track, and I doubt whether a more suitable place could have been found than that which was finally chosen—a section between Sears Crossing signal gantry and Bridego Bridge—about half a mile from the gantry, where the railway embankment runs down from the track to the roadway.

Finally, a search had to be made for a base from which to operate and that could be used as a hide-out before and after

the robbery, where the gang could come and go without at-
tracting attention, and on the night of the holdup leave late,
carry out the robbery, and then go back and lie low until it was
safe for them to break up and go their different ways.

It must have taken some time to find exactly what they
wanted, but eventually towards the end of July they had the
good fortune to discover Leatherslade Farm—an ideal place
for their needs, about fifteen miles from Bridego Bridge—
which was being offered for sale.

Looking at the thing in a detached way, one had to admit
that the operation was perfectly planned and carried out. Indeed, except for the unnecessary violence inflicted on the
driver, it was a crime almost without flaw, comparable in its
way to one of the commando raids during the Second World
War. Besides the detailed planning that was essential to the
robbery's success, funds were needed beforehand to cover the
expenses involved—to pay for information, for extensive
bribery, and for a large deposit on the purchase of the farm.
According to information that I received the robbery was
financed from the proceeds of the wages snatch at London
Airport in November 1962, when a gang seized £62,000 that
was being delivered to the offices there. The accuracy of this
information was later to be confirmed by Wilson in 1968, in a
Sunday newspaper after he had been recaptured, following his
escape from prison.

The robbers having completed their plans, it became obvious
that it would be necessary to recruit some more men for the
rapid unloading of the mail bags. So a few days before the
robbery, a small number of men belonging to criminal circles
in south London, who were chosen with care and in whom
every confidence could be placed, were approached and told
just so much about the plan and no more. On agreeing to join
the enterprise, they were instructed to go to Leatherslade
Farm, making their way their singly, so as not to attract the
attention of the locals. Thus a first-class team was built up and
each man briefed to do his particular job speedily and effi-
ciently.

Shortly before the robbery was due to take place a preliminary operation was performed. Although it was later suspected that there might have been some tampering with three vans specially built for carrying HVP, we could find no proof of this at the time. However, Mrs. Wilson in one of her newspaper articles confirmed that our suspicions were correct. The vans were put out of action so as to ensure that an older and less secure type of van without corridor access to the following coach would be in use for the Glasgow–Euston run on the night of August 7–8.

The Goddess of Luck conferred one inestimable favor upon the robbers. Just for a short period before and after the holdup the weather was beautiful, and on the night in question it was warm and still with a clear starry sky. As members of the gang arrived they were no doubt taken to Bridego Bridge, shown the terrain and fully briefed on the tactics of the operation.

On the night there were altogether thirteen men at the farm and I was told that at about midnight they were joined by Douglas Goody. He reported that he had had a telephone call —there was no telephone at the farm—from someone in the North who was in on the job to say that the train was carrying the money as anticipated and was running according to schedule.

A little later, dressed in boiler suits and woolen helmets with eye slits, the whole gang moved off and later split into two sections—one going to a point near the signal gantry at Sears Crossing, and the other to Bridego Bridge, where on the road beside the embankment the lorry and the two Land Rovers were parked.

In the first group was Roger Cordrey, whose job was to deal with the signals; with him were two men to uncouple the HVP coach from the rest of the train, and a number of others armed with pickaxe handles, who were to overpower the engine driver and fireman. What happened subsequently has already been described.

With Boal, Cordrey, and the others who had been arrested, Charles Wilson was lodged in Bedford Gaol and during the preliminary hearings, which were at Linslade Magistrates'

Court some twenty miles away, he was taken there once a week, escorted by prison officers, in a police van. Shortly after Wilson's arrest I received information that a plan was being made to ambush the van and rescue him. The times of the journey, the route, the traffic frequency, all these things had been carefully studied and a fast getaway arranged. Brigadier Cheney, when I told him this, arranged for a strong police escort, but eventually, as more and more people were arrested, a section of Aylesbury Prison (normally a women's prison) was reserved for the prisoners and the plans laid by Wilson's friends were set aside. This does not mean that they were by any means abandoned, as we shall shortly see.

A few days after the robbery, and consequently before we had a clue as to the men we were looking for, a man and a woman had called on a couple living near Reigate in Surrey, who had advertised a camping vehicle for sale. The man, who gave the name of Ballard, agreed to the price, £325, and paid it in £5 and £1 notes. Later in the day, the previous owners called to collect some things they had left in the caravan and on this occasion saw, besides Ballard and his wife, a child, and a white poodle.

During the next few days it was noticed at various shops in Reigate that a woman was paying some quite sizable bills with £5 and £1 notes. By this time, following the enormous publicity in the press, people were ready to regard anyone possessing large sums in cash with suspicion. After paying £26 at a dress shop, this woman was watched by the manageress, who saw her go into two other shops and then join a man waiting in a car. The manageress took the number of the car and telephoned the police. The car was spotted in Reigate shortly afterwards and the driver was questioned. He was alone at the time, but while the police were talking to him, he was joined by a woman with a child and a white poodle. The name given by the man, and which was on his driving license, was James Patton. The answers he gave to the police seemed satisfactory, so they did not detain him.

When, soon after this, photographs of the wanted men and descriptions of them and their families were published, the police who had stopped Ballard, and various shop assistants in Reigate, all recognized him as James White. The caravan still at the site where he had been living was searched, and £30,440 was found hidden in the paneling. Fingerprints which were also found were identified as White's. A full-scale search was mounted, and in a house which he had formerly occupied were found some bank-note wrappers identifiable as part of the proceeds of the robbery, but no trace was found of White or his family.

With all the information I had at this point there was not much left for me to do in the way of planning. There were still conferences to attend with the Director of Public Prosecutions and Crown counsel, but I had picked a very strong team of CID officers and had allotted them specific tasks, so except for conferring every day with the leaders of the team, I felt it best to let them get on with the job. Nothing can be more disturbing to the concentration and initiative of a detective investigating a case than to feel that a superior officer is breathing down his neck.

The arrest of Wheater and the Fields brought the total of suspects charged in connection with the robbery up to eleven. The identification of fingerprints found at the farm meant that we still had five more to find: James, Daly, Edwards, Reynolds, and White. Daly was the first to be discovered, early in December 1963. He was living in a flat in Belgravia.

The arrest of Roy James a few days later, in contrast with the more formal proceedings when the others were arrested, provided something of a sensation. James' name and address was among those I had been given shortly after the robbery. Consequently, on August 22 detectives went to his flat in Chelsea, but inquiries showed that he had not been there for several days. It was not until nearly four months later, on December 10 that news was received that he was living in a flat in St. John's Wood.

In searches that had been made at places where some of the other missing men had been living, it was found that all sorts of arrangements had been made for them to escape—by rope ladders, roof-top routes, and so on. Mr. Butler decided to take no chances. Direct observation of James' flat was impossible because it was in a mews where there was no chance of concealment and at the back were gardens that offered ideal opportunities for escape. So Mr. Butler got an Ordnance Survey map of the area and noted on it every possible point of access to the mews. He then posted about thirty officers at these particular spots and when everything was ready a woman detective went to the flat, ostensibly to deliver a parcel. She knocked, but got no answer, though she could hear someone moving about inside. Then two officers climbed to a first-floor balcony and got in by smashing a window. As they did so, they saw James making off through a skylight. They followed him over the roofs down the full length of the mews where he jumped into the arms of a deputation waiting to welcome him.

He was carrying a holdall which had some £12,000 in it and in an envelope that he had on him was another £130 odd. The money in the holdall included two £5 notes whose serial numbers were among the few that had been recorded. These, with James' fingerprints found on articles at the farm, provided overwhelming evidence against him.

James' arrest fell short of what Mr. Butler had hoped for. The information we had been given was that James was expecting a visit that evening from Bruce Reynolds, so it was decided to leave some officers in the flat to wait for him. Unfortunately, someone had been quick to tell the newspapers about what had been going on in the mews and the place soon became filled with reporters and photographers, who hung about in the hope of further developments. One look at them must have told Reynolds, if in fact he ever turned up, that it would be best for him to stay away.

An hour or so before all this happened, Mr. Butler had had an anonymous telephone call from someone who said that if he would go to a telephone kiosk at Black Horse Court in Southwark, he would find something of interest. He went there and discovered two potato sacks crammed with bank notes which were found to amount to £47,254. Fifty-seven of the notes were identifiable by their serial numbers as having come from a bank in Scotland. Though both the sacks and the notes were scientifically examined at the Laboratory, nothing was found to indicate who had been handling them.

Why these notes were dumped in this way is open to speculation. My own theory is this: such very large quantities of notes could not possibly have been hidden in a house or flat so as to avoid discovery if the place were searched, and certainly could not have been paid into any bank at that particular time without suspicion being aroused. Among the men whose descriptions I had been given, though I did not know their names, was one about whom extensive inquiries were made and who in fact was interrogated at length. But in spite of our strong suspicions, nothing could be proved against him and so no charge could be brought. My belief is that he thought we knew a lot more about him than we did, and thinking things were getting too hot, he decided to get rid of the money to avoid being found in possession of it. Had there been any evidence to substantiate our suspicions, he, obviously, would have been the fourteenth member of the gang.

The robbers' trial began at Aylesbury under Mr. (now Lord) Edmund Justice Davies on January 20, 1964. Up till this time the longest trial in British criminal history—it lasted thirty-three days—was the Fire Raising case in 1933, in which I had also been concerned. Nineteen defendants and 150 witnesses were involved and more than 600 exhibits produced. The Train Robbers' trial lasted almost three months, from January 20, to April 16, 1964. In all, there were nineteen defendants, including relatives and associates of the men accused of actually doing the job, who were implicated in various ways. Witnesses and exhibits were both considerably more numerous and nearly forty counsel were involved.

The task of the police in preparing the case was enormous. Multiple copies of some hundreds of documents and exhibits had to be made for judge, jury, and counsel and so arranged as to be available at a moment's notice. An army of witnesses had to be alerted, some coming from as far afield as Scotland, and arrangements made for each of them to appear at the right time on the right day. These witnesses included bank officials, postal and railway workers, police officers, scientific and technical witnesses, fingerprint experts, and a very large number of people who had been interviewed during the inquiries. It is a high tribute to the police that on the whole arrangements for the trial functioned smoothly. The only "incident" was a telephone call to one of the jurors from a friend of some of the accused, who intimated that it would be worth the juror's while if they were found not guilty. This caller's identity was never established.

Towards the end of the trial one of the chief defendants, John Daly, was acquitted. Although his fingerprints had been found on a set of Monopoly tokens at the farm, the judge ruled that their discovery implied no more than suspicion against him. Daly did not deny that the fingerprints were his, but it was stated in his defense he had only played Monopoly with friends in London and was unable to account for these tokens having been found at the farm.

Seven of the accused, Biggs, Goody, Hussey, James, Welch, Wilson, and Wisbey, received sentences of thirty years' imprisonment; the two Fields, twenty-five years each; Boal, twenty-four years; Cordrey, twenty years; and Wheater, three years. All except Wheater and the Fields had previous criminal convictions.

Later that day, after they had been sentenced, one woman and five men appeared before the Court charged with receiving various amounts of the stolen money. No evidence was offered by the prosecution against the woman and one of the men, and they were discharged. Two of the others were given conditional discharges; a fourth, who pleaded guilty to receiving £2,000, was sentenced to three years; the fifth man, who admitted receiving £518, was sentenced to one year.

At the end of the trial Mr. Justice Davies made a speech of some length in praise of the immense and tireless efforts of the many police officers who had been concerned in the case. For my part, no praise could be too high for the officers in all ranks of the Flying Squad, who had arrested all those who were charged, except Cordrey and Boal. Every day for six weeks after the robbery they worked often from sixteen to twenty hours a day, snatching a few hours' sleep when they could at the Yard, so that during this time their wives and families saw little of them.

As was to be expected in a case involving such heavy sentences, several of those who had been convicted decided to appeal. The sentences on Cordrey and Boal were reduced to fourteen years and those on the two Fields to five years.

Convicted prisoners have the right, of which they almost always take advantage, to attend the Court of Appeal, and are brought to the Law Courts in London from whatever prison they have been sent to. Wilson, who had gone to Winson Green Prison in Birmingham, said somewhat surprisingly that he did not want to go to court to hear his appeal.

Winson Green was built about 1840, and like most English prisons of that period, is hopelessly out of date as a penal establishment. It is also, like most prisons, badly understaffed. On the night of August 12, 1964, several men scaled the prison's outer wall with ladders and made their way unobserved to the block where Wilson's cell was. On their way they opened various doors with keys which they had somehow obtained, and when they reached the block they overpowered the officer on duty and gagged and bound him. Then, having got Wilson out of his cell, they left the prison by the same route, observing prison rules by carefully locking all doors behind them. It was obvious, of course, why Wilson had not wished to go to London for his appeal—his rescue, planned almost immediately after the trial, had been arranged to take place at that time. From the moment of his escape, Wilson, with his wife and two children, vanished into the blue.

One other member of the gang, Ronald Biggs, also escaped from prison. The circumstances were no less sensational than those of Wilson's get away, but there were elements of comedy about the episode that reminded one of a Keystone Cops film. Biggs, who had nine previous convictions, was transferred, in spite of his record, from a provincial jail to Wandsworth Prison, another Victorian establishment which could hardly be regarded as offering maximum security. In Wandsworth, Biggs found himself among old friends, one of whom, Eric Flowers, he had known since boyhood. What passed between them is not known, but plans for his escape must have begun almost immediately. Shortly after being released, his friend, with two members of his family, bought an old furniture van which they converted to their purpose by cutting a hole in the roof and installing a makeshift lift inside. The friend knew, of course, the time at which Biggs would be exercising in the prison yard and one afternoon while he was there the van was driven to the prison and parked alongside a deserted part of the outer wall. Two men wearing stocking masks went up on the lift to the top of the wall, twenty-five feet from the ground, and threw a flexible ladder down into the yard. Biggs, who was waiting below, immediately ran to it and climbed up, followed by Flowers, whom he had invited to join them. Two other prisoners gate-crashed the party and followed them. From the wall they jumped through the hole in the van's roof, landed on a mattress, and then scrambled out and into a car alongside the van, in which they all drove away. Seven men were involved altogether, of whom all but Biggs and Flowers were soon traced and arrested, thanks to one of the rescue team running off with the sister of his wife, who showed her disapproval by informing the police. Biggs and Flowers, like Wilson, both disappeared into the blue.

One thing puzzled me for a long time, and that was the gang's failure to remove evidence of the occupation of the farm. I could not understand such apparent stupidity after the careful and elaborate preparations that had been made to ensure the success of the robbery itself. However, I was told during the inquiry that someone had been paid a considerable sum of money to burn the farm down after the gang had left. This final move had been planned no less carefully than the rest of the crime. Those responsible had not only gone to the trouble of finding out how long it would take the fire brigade to get to the farm, but even to examine the hydrant in the road some quarter of a mile away to see whether the brigade's hoses would fit it. According to my information they found this was not possible.

If this final operation had been carried out according to plan, there is little doubt that with the destruction of the gang's finger- and palmprints we should have finished up, as often happens in the case of a big robbery, knowing perfectly well the identity of most of those concerned, but unable to produce evidence with which to support a charge. Why the man who was detailed to do the job failed to carry out his instructions, only he can say. The probability is that he decided the risk of being discovered setting the place on fire was too great for him to wait behind and finish the job off. If success in a criminal investigation depends surprisingly often on a little piece of luck, this time we were handed a large slice.

When the trail ended in April 1964, White, Edwards, and Reynolds were still at large. Mr. Butler, whom I saw from time to time after I retired, seemed in his own quiet way confident that he would eventually bring them to justice and that Wilson and Biggs would be recaptured.

After two and a half years, White decided to give himself up. I do no know what his reason was, but I suspect there was not much hush money left. Criminals, especially those in the protection racket, can be just as hard on each other as they are on society. There was no evidence that White had much money left, though as a result of information that he gave to the police, another £7,000 odd was found. White was tried in June 1966 and received a sentence of eighteen years.

Ronald Edwards was eventually traced, after a very long and painstaking investigation, through his fingerprints being found on a car used by a business firm with which he had become connected. None of his dividends from the robbery were forthcoming. He was tried and convicted in December 1966 and sent to prison for fifteen years.

In 1967 Mr. Butler traced Wilson to a small town in the province of Quebec, where he was living with his wife and two children. Mr. Butler went there with some officers of the Royal Canadian Mounted Police and Wilson was re-arrested and brought back to England to serve the rest of his sentence.

At the end of 1967, Mr. Butler was due to retire, but was asked to stay on at the Yard for another year. It was a year well spent. Towards the end of it, on November 8, 1968, he brought to a successful conclusion his prolonged and tenacious efforts to find Bruce Reynolds by tracing him to a house at Torquay in Devonshire, where he had been living for two months under the name of Hillier. Butler arrested him in an early morning raid, and in due course Reynolds was placed on trial. He pleaded guilty and was sentenced to twenty-five years' imprisonment.

During the time the police had been searching for him, Reynolds, with his wife and son, had been on the move in various parts of Europe, as well as in Mexico, the United States, and Canada. Mr. Butler followed his movements all this time, but until he reached Torquay had always been just too late in pinpointing his whereabouts. When Reynolds returned to England he had little left to show for his criminal efforts. All he possessed was about £6,000, and, unlike any of the other robbers, he offered this as restitution.

This brought the total of money recovered to £349,000—less than one seventh of the amount stolen, which was £2,595,997 10s. 0d.

It seemed that this was the final episode in the long, sordid and brutal story of the Great Train Robbery. But in October 1969 news came of the discovery of Ronald Biggs and his friend Flowers in Melbourne, Australia. But, as Reynolds had so often done, Biggs managed to keep one jump ahead of the police and disappeared before they could arrest him. At the time of writing he is still at large. Flowers, however, who had also gone there with him, was located in Sydney, re-arrested and brought back to England to finish a twelve-year sentence for armed robbery.

The life of a hunted man can never be anything but a life of fear and anxiety; but perhaps there is some compensation for Biggs in knowing that his wife, like Charles Wilson's, was allowed to turn her knowledge of his crime to advantage by supplying her story to a newspaper and being well paid for so doing.

Less well rewarded for his pains was the train driver, Jack Mills, who in trying to protect the mail and defend himself was so severely beaten up that he never fully recovered from the effects of the attack. It was not until shortly before his death from leukemia in February 1970 that the public became aware of his straitened circumstances and a subscription was raised for him. But it was too late for him to have much benefit from it.

No words of mine could provide a more appropriate epilogue to the greatest robbery of all time than those spoken by Mr. Justice Davies at the trial: "Let us clear out of the way any romantic notions of dare-devilry. This is nothing less than a sordid crime of violence inspired by greed."

About the Author

George Hatherill served in France and Flanders during the First World War in a London territorial regiment. Equipped by this experience with an excellent grasp of French and German, he joined the Special Branch of the British police, and five years later was sent to Brussels to serve as liaison officer with the Belgian police. Between his transfer to the CID (Scotland Yard) in 1931 and the outbreak of World War II he frequently worked abroad investigating a variety of cases. In 1939 he was back in France with the British Army setting up a system to reduce looting of army supplies.

After the War he was in charge of various sections of the CID, was for a time second in command of the police of a quarter of London, and from 1954 to his retirement in 1964 he was Commander of the CID (a post now called Deputy Assistant Commissioner). A lecturer on English criminal investigation methods and criminal law in several European countries, the United States, and Canada, Hatherill was awarded the CBE in 1964.